A SUSSEX GUIDE

THE COUNTY OF SUSSEX

CATWICK · EAST GRINSTEAD · RYE

HORSHAM · HAYWARDS HEATH · HASTINGS

MIDHURST · CHICHESTER · HEATHFIELD · LEWES · EASTBOURNE

WORTHING · BRIGHTON

A23 · A272 · A265 · A259 · A27

ENGLISH CHANNEL

A TOUR ALONG
THE SUSSEX
COAST

DAVID ARSCOTT

INTRODUCED BY
CLIVE ASLET

Illustrated by
IVAN HISSEY

SNAKE RIVER PRESS

SNAKE RIVER PRESS

Book No 18
Books about Sussex for the enthusiast

Published in 2008 by
SNAKE RIVER PRESS
South Downs Way, Alfriston, Sussex BN26 5XW
www.snakeriverpress.co.uk

ISBN 978-1-906022-17-4

This book was conceived, designed and produced by
SNAKE RIVER PRESS

ART DIRECTOR & PUBLISHER *Peter Bridgewater*
EDITORIAL DIRECTOR *Viv Croot*
EDITOR *Robert Yarham*
PAGE MAKEUP *Richard Constable & Chris Morris*
ILLUSTRATOR *Ivan Hissey*
CONSULTANT *Lorraine Harrison*

This book is typeset in Perpetua & Gill Sans,
two fonts designed by Eric Gill

Printed and bound in China

———

DEDICATION

For Rosie, Jack & Beth

my flotsam & jetsam

CONTENTS

FOREWORD

My mother was born in Chichester. One of my earliest memories is of our paraffin-smelling beach hut on the sands at West Wittering – an indistinct memory, associated with windbreaks, shrimping and huddling besides groynes. When my grandmother moved away, we stopped going, but a watercolour of Bosham, showing a horse and cart making its slow progress across the estuary, with the church – which also appears in the Bayeux tapestry – to one side, hung in our dining room. For me, these early associations impart a special glow to Sussex by the sea.

Later, I made a radio programme about Bailiffscourt, near Littlehampton: a medievalising house that incorporates fragments of genuinely ancient architecture, designed by an antiquarian for Lord and Lady Moyne, before World War II. An early champion of wildflower meadows, Lady Moyne used to travel down from London by train, throwing wild flower seed out of the windows – much to the chagrin of her husband, who was Minister of Agriculture at the time. I also helped the late Lord Bessborough (who stayed at Bailiffscourt in its heyday, buzzing his friends on what was then the new fangled inter-room telephone) supplement a book on his home Stansted Park, just on the Sussex side of the Hampshire border, a house peopled through the centuries by a singular parade of characters – dukes, opera singers, nabobs, a converter of the Jews, John Keats (he visited), a successful wine merchant, finally the Bessboroughs themselves. More recently I have spent happy afternoons in Winchelsea, beloved of the Pre-Raphaelites, and Alfriston, where the Clergy House is the first building owned by the National Trust; at the Napoleonic redoubt in Eastbourne; walking beside the meanders of the Cuckmere Valley; wondering at the long history of Pevensey Castle; finding myself forever astonished by the super-heated luxury of the Prince Regent's Brighton Pavilion.

There is variety aplenty on the Sussex coast. It can be seen in the buildings – flint walls bump up against brick ones, before tumbling downhill (if the town is Rye) in a succession of tilehanging and half timber. The majestic, stucco-fronted terraces of Brighton and Hove shrug their shoulders at the chaotic development of Peacehaven. Architectural variety is only part of it, though. It reflects another quality. As David Arscott admirably demonstrates in this volume, individuality flourishes on the Sussex coast. Perhaps it was something to do with the pattern of landownership, broken down into yeoman parcels rather than aggregated into big estates; or the independent nature of fishing communities. Thriving on the fortnightly change of visitors in seaside resorts, it has been fertile ground for bohemian seeds to sprout in; a natural home to people who don't quite fit in elsewhere. Only in Lewes could a flat-sharer be sought to join 'three non-smoking vegetarian ceramicists'. Hurrah for the shingly, Martello towerish, lighthouse-protected, chalk-cliffed, fresh-crab personality of the Sussex coast, so joyfully celebrated in this book: how many childhoods would be short on memories without it?

CLIVE ASLET

INTRODUCTION

Here leaps ashore the full Sou'west
All heavy-winged with brine,
Here lies above the foldest crest
The channel's leaden line;
And here the sea-fogs lap and cling,
And here, each warning each,
The sheep-bells and the ship-bells ring
Along the hidden beach

RUDYARD KIPLING *SUSSEX, 1902*

In an age when proximity to the sea is likely to add several thousand pounds to the value of a property, it's difficult to believe that the wealthy once built their houses to face in precisely the opposite direction. To them, it seems, the ocean was not a thing of beauty, and the winds that drove ashore from it were ominous rather than bracing and invigorating.

This is a useful reminder at the beginning of a 'seaside' book which is certainly not confined to the bucket-and-spade imagery that phrase so readily conjures up. Tourism came relatively late to Sussex, and although our journey west from the sand dunes of Camber will take in piers and promenades, marinas and amusements, it will also discover evidence of a much wider range of human activity along the coastline over the centuries. Indeed, through the fossil record we shall be taken back to a time well before *homo sapiens* ever set foot here.

One recurring theme is the powerlessness of man against the elements. The earliest trace of a human ancestor in Sussex is the shin bone of Boxgrove Man, who foraged along what was then the shingle foreshore some 500,000 years ago. Consult your map and you'll see that the site is today about 6 miles (10 km) inland. Over the millennia the sea level has risen and fallen dramatically, the chalk Downs themselves formed below the waters and later thrust up above them by a mighty clashing of subterranean tectonic plates. The restless waves finally cut off southern England from mainland Europe around 8,000 years ago, and they have tormented the inhabitants of our island ever since – at times swamping the land, at others sullenly withdrawing. Sea walls and groynes speak of our relatively feeble attempts to resist their ravagings, while Rye and Winchelsea (Kipling's 'ports of stranded pride') are ancient trading towns helplessly beached by the receding tides.

And then the shipwrecks: in shallow water between Camber and Cuckmere Haven can be found what Peter Marsden, a leading authority on the subject, has described as 'an exceptional concentration of historical shipwrecks that can be visited by non-divers at suitable low tides'. These vessels, which foundered from the 17th to the 20th centuries, between them chart the story of shipbuilding development 'from wood and sail to steel and engine'. Graveyards all along our coast have memorials to those lost at sea – among them the 17 brave lifeboatmen of Rye Harbour who perished together in the disaster of 1928.

To many, of course, the sea has brought prosperity. In medieval times Hastings was an original member of the Confederation of Cinque Ports which helped protect the realm against invasion in the days before the Royal Navy, and other Sussex coastal towns later joined it. We still have working ports at Newhaven and Shoreham, and although our fishing industry is much depleted and predominantly inshore, there are still some 300 boats registered here. For the lack of natural harbours the fishermen at Hastings and Worthing have to launch their vessels from the beach, while those at Selsey use offshore moorings. Brighton had its foreshore washed away long ago (it was a decayed former fishing town when the Prince Regent first knew it), but has its modern marina to offer instead.

Illegal trading has also been a prominent feature of coastal life, and the smugglers were not always furtive. In November 1744, for instance, three large cutters unloaded contraband at Pevensey Bay, with 500 packhorses mustered to carry it inland, and it's been estimated that at one time as much as a quarter of the nation's overseas trade was being shipped in on the sly. There are memorials to 'free traders' in Sussex graveyards and a stone in Chichester recording the spot where six of them were hanged, but the most obvious monuments to their activities are the coastguard cottages and watch houses which survive in raised positions overlooking the beaches.

Its island status has spared Britain from successful invasion since 1066, but this has been no God-given immunity. Sussex has always been at the front line in times of trouble, and our perambulations will reveal the extent and variety of the defences that have been erected along our coast over the centuries to keep enemies at bay – from a mound thrown up at Pevensey Castle to house a cannon against the Spanish Armada, through a range of Napoleonic fortifications to tank traps from World War II.

Peaceful incursions have been much more common: indeed, no county can have been more criss-crossed than Sussex by people on their way between London and the continent. Holiday-making, and day-tripping in the case of Brighton especially, have made a major impact on our coastline, as has the desire of huge numbers of people to retire to an area that promises fresh air, open skies and the memory of times innocently spent. From Winchelsea Beach to Shoreham Beach, Felpham, Pagham and West Wittering, converted railway carriages – sometimes pebble dashed, with rows of small windows the only clue to their origins – are remnants of come-as-you-are beach communities largely cleared away by the army during the last war. We shan't dwell on the rash of bungalow development and caravan parks we pass (although the story of Peacehaven demands to be told), but we must acknowledge that Cuckmere Haven is the one rivermouth to have been spared development and that the lovely switchback of downland between it and Beachy Head is a Sussex rarity in being an unspoilt stretch of countryside next to the sea.

Against the drab and the dismal, however, we must set the bold, bright and beautiful. Keith Waterhouse famously described Brighton as a town constantly helping the police with their enquiries, and in similar vein the coast in general might be personified as a lively schoolboy constantly playing truant. A saunter along the front encourages a footloose, fancy-free demeanour, and normal rules don't quite apply. This is a place to have fun. Even architects are affected by a heady spirit of adventure, designing buildings which are fanciful in themselves or which have no need to fit into their surroundings other than by being eye-catching: the glassy, modernist De La Warr Pavilion at Bexhill; Prinnie's oriental Royal Pavilion at Brighton with its domes, turrets and over-the-top interiors; the recent East Beach Café at Littlehampton, an open shell created from plates of patinated steel.

The guiding principle of this book has been to record interesting things discovered within sight and smell of the sea. It's not a conventional 'walks guide', leading you step by step and stile by stile – indeed, I have little doubt that most readers will drive or take public transport to some of the sites before lacing up their boots. I warmly recommend the six Ordnance Survey Explorer maps numbers 120-125, which will help you decide whether to follow my east-west route with dogged devotion or, instead, to devise shortcuts or diversions to suit your own whim.

Sussex is 76 miles (122 km) east to west, and a meandering exploration of the coast will increase that distance by some little length, so our journey is best approached in leisurely stages. (I have created 20 of them.) Along the way we shall explore a little geology and a little natural history, but especially the impact of our human activities on the coastal fringes of Sussex. The variety is as exhilarating as a gust of tangy air in your face as you walk along the prom.

AT THE END OF THE WORLD

CAMBER TO RYE HARBOUR

I t's a twisting route from the foothills of Rye to Camber Sands, out over East Guldeford Level, an outlier of Romney Marsh, with sheep in their hundreds on one hand, deep, water-filled gravel pits on the other and a sky that seems to go on for ever. This is where Sussex begins and ends – at first acquaintance with a whimper.

If you thought the Isle of Wight was the last word in *passé* bucket-and-spade English holiday-making, hone your vocabulary for little Camber. It still has a barracks-like holiday camp, for goodness sake, while just along the main road you'll find a well appointed launderette to alert you to the meagreness of the facilities in many of the flimsy holiday lets that sprawl untidily all about you.

Sea Road, whose name lures the pedestrian following the salt scent in his nostrils, is nothing but a track of loose sand among plain bunga-lows. A cul-de-sac off to the left has its name hand-written in desperate capitals – First Avenue – while the sign to the next turning (Second Avenue, of course) has faded almost beyond decipherment. Perhaps the postman never calls.

You are led at last to the car park most day visitors will use, a large space jostled by buildings that cater for your every immediate need: there are cafés majoring in 'donuts', fish 'n' chips and ice creams, an amusement arcade ('These premises are alarmed') and a beach shop selling inflatables, windbreaks, sunhats, suncream and all the other paraphernalia suitable for an experience which feels, at the moment, little more than fantasy. And then the sands! Beyond a protective ring of extensive dunes, bound together by marram grass and sea buckthorn, lies a vast expanse of dimpled softness, descending gradually, safely to the lapping wavelets. On a warm early September day, at the fag-end of the season, there are but a few families here by mid-morning, their little ones scampering naked in the sunshine. This is the coast as freedom. Turn your back on the tawdry civilisation behind you and there's only the sand beneath your toes (a rare commodity in Sussex) and the pure sea stretching out to a distant horizon.

Ignore the ugly, steaming bulk of the nuclear power station at Dungeness to the east – it's over the border in Kent and doesn't concern us. Here there is only tranquillity. Gulls bob on the sea in huge numbers, terns, even this late in the season, plummet for fish and a lone little egret steps delicately through a shallow pool.

Old Winchelsea

But this area has another tale to tell – of the power of the sea and man's helplessness against its fury. Somewhere off these sands, so far gone as to be untraceable, lie the ruins of old Winchelsea. It sat on a shingle spit here, and some seven centuries ago it was completely washed away by violent storms and turbulent waters which had been greedily devouring the coastline, acre by acre, over several generations.

This was no tiny fishing village of huddled cottages but one of the major trading ports of southern England. It had been a royal dockyard in King John's days, and was a leading member of the Confederation of Cinque Ports which provided men and ships for the monarch in return for special privileges amounting almost to independence. When its destruction by natural forces became inevitable, Edward I sanctioned the building of a replacement port a few miles away on the hill of Iham. We shall visit it later – and discover how the sea still managed to have the last laugh.

Now, though, we take a half-hour's stroll west across the sands to the River Rother. Look across the fast-running water and you see a rather different landscape beyond. Here, against a rising backdrop of green hills, is a world of shingle – bank after bank of it stretching away, with a glimpse of an ancient sandstone castle among its folds.

To reach it we must retrace our steps, drive back across the flatlands to Rye and take the road down to Rye Harbour.

The Mary Stanford disaster

As you approach the village of Rye Harbour through an industrial estate that could win an international prize for grimness, you'll see the Victorian Church of the Holy Spirit on your right. An extension in 1912 was roofed to resemble an upturned boat – a ghastly portent of the fate that was to befall the local lifeboat a mere 16 years later. This was a village that earned its living from the sea. It had, of course, lost its share of young men in the Great War, and now another 17 would perish in a catastrophe that need never have happened.

It was at about 6.45 on the morning of November 15th that the lifeboat, the *Mary Stanford*, was launched from the beach in atrocious weather to rescue the crew of a Latvian steamer which had collided with a German ship off Dungeness. Even to reach the remote boathouse the men had to struggle for well over a mile from their homes against the driving wind and rain, and then they had to haul the boat manually over the shingle. The conditions were so bad that they failed to spot the Verey lights which, almost immediately, were fired to recall them: the steamer's crew had already been taken safely aboard the German vessel. Some four hours later, with no let-up in the storm, the lifeboat was on her way back into Rye Harbour when she was overturned by a monstrous wave. It was the worst disaster in British lifeboat history.

In the churchyard is a substantial memorial to the men who died, several of them related (the coxwain had his two sons on board) and all of them well known to everyone in what was then a very small community. The inscription reads: 'We have done that which was our duty to do'. Inside the church there is a large plaque to the men's memory and another which lists the 128 lives saved by the local lifeboat since 1852.

Martello towers

The road ends a few hundred yards further on from the church, and now it's time to walk or cycle. By the car park is the first of several Martello towers we shall meet on our travels. This is in truth a sorry example (boarded up, sprouting vegetation and sporting fierce 'Keep Out' notices), but its very survival speaks a truth about their durability: no fewer than 45 of them survive, if sometimes precariously. You'll find them all along the south-east coast from Aldeburgh in Suffolk to Seaford – the easternmost in a chain of 103 completed in 1812. Built of brick, and with their outer walls 30-ft (9-m) thick, they were designed to keep Napoleon at bay should he attempt an invasion. They were inspired by a similarly round tower at Cape Mortella in Corsica, which the Royal Navy had attacked with great difficulty a few years before. Although it's suggested that the name we use arose from a confusion with the Italian coastal watch towers known as *torres di martello*, I prefer to think that a naval secretary simply took a poor shorthand note.

Rye Harbour Nature Reserve

A stone's throw from the tower is the distinctly understated entrance to one of the finest nature reserves in the county. The path at first runs alongside the Rother, then turns west among the serried shingle banks we observed from the other side of the river. Together with those to the east at Dungeness they form the largest coastal shingle feature in Europe, with a hardy vegetation of sea kale, sea pea, viper's bugloss and yellow horned poppy and, in the spring, a nesting congregation of little terns, common terns, oystercatchers and ringed plovers.

For the birder, indeed, this is a place for all seasons. Apart from the shingle there are areas of reedbed and several former gravel pits which have become freshwater lakes. On my first visit to the largest of them, Castle Water, all binoculars and telescopes in the hide were trained on a visiting osprey which had, a little too soon for me, recently swooped down to take a pike.

There are three signposted walks, all on the flat and the longest taking about three hours. For this, we turn inland soon after passing the former *Mary Stanford* boathouse (never used again after the disaster) and resisting the temptation to continue to Winchelsea Beach, which we shall visit later.

The shingle is largely grass-covered now, as we pass through scrub and low woodland, skirt the edge of Castle Water and come face to face with the ruined fortification after which it is named.

Camber Castle

If the question hasn't occurred to you before, it surely will when you step inside the castle: why does it stand in such a strange place, a good mile from the bay it was supposed to protect? The answer is that it was indeed overlooking the water when Henry VIII had it built – one of several 'Henrican' artillery forts (the others all in Kent) designed to repel any French or Spanish attempt at invasion. The shingle banks over which we have just walked were brought in by the sea, decade by decade, over hundreds of years.

Work on the castle began in 1539, but by the end of the century the silting of the harbour and the eastward shift of its entrance were already making it obsolete. In short, its cannon were no longer able to fire their shot far enough to trouble enemy shipping, and in 1637 the garrison was disbanded.

Although much of the castle was at one time damaged and filled in, it's the only one of Henry's forts not to have been subsequently modified, which means that you can get a good idea of what it was like in its brief heyday. English Heritage began putting it to rights in the 1960s, and it's now open on weekend afternoons in the season. There are warnings about dark tunnels with limited headroom and of places where there's a long drop, but mercifully the safety-first brigade hasn't gone mad at Camber Castle, and you can explore to your heart's content.

❯ While making the return journey from Camber to Rye, take the very short diversion on the A259 Folkestone Road to East Guldeford. Here's a church with a difference, and not only because of the box pews inside. It stands in isolation in the marshes, is one of only three in Sussex made of Tudor brick and looks every bit like a twin-roofed barn.

A HILLTOP SURVIVOR

RYE

There's a confusion of waterways below the hill on which Rye stands. At Strand Quay the little River Tillingham arrives jauntily enough from its starting point up in the High Weald to flow past the old, black weatherboarded warehouses and to keep afloat (when the tide is in, at least) a veritable flotilla of pleasure boats. Almost immediately, however, it surrenders its name to the slightly larger River Brede which, approaching from the flatlands to the west, meets it at a sluice close to the Martello tower. This triumph is itself short-lived, for the Rother promptly sweeps down from the north past the town's eastern flank and swallows the Brede on its route to the sea.

This riverine drama is played out a full 2 miles (3.2 km) from the narrow harbour mouth we overlooked at Camber Sands. The longshore drift, which built up the prodigious shingle banks in front of Camber Castle, ruined Rye as a trading port at the end of the 16th century and it still tests the resolve and expertise of the harbour authorities today. Each year some 55,000 tons of the stuff have to be removed – and even this Sisyphean labour allows sailors an access window of only two or three hours either side of high tide – while up by Strand Quay the Environment Agency has begun so-called hydrodynamic dredging in order to keep the channel clear. The trick is to pump seawater into the thick deposits of silt so that they disperse and filter out on the tide to swell the existing mudflats alongside the estuary.

While we're down at the quay, let's confront what it is that some people don't like about Rye. In a nutshell, it's the quaint, smug, over-preserved face it presents to the visitor. True, there's a thriving fishing fleet on the Rother, around the corner at the Salts, but here there are expensive gin-and-tonic craft where once there was a shipbuilding industry and where, when Rye was one of the mighty Cinque Ports, great merchant vessels from northern Europe unloaded their treasures. Today the warehouses have become upmarket restaurants and antique shops. The Heritage Centre, although it houses the excellent *son-et-lumière* town model, is little more than an anodyne gewgaw shop. It's typical, the critic would say, that the skeleton in its cage which tells the story of the murderer Breeds (more later) is fake. What actually survives is the top of his skull in the original gibbet, now kept in an attic room at the town hall but no longer on general view: I've seen it, and it's genuinely grisly.

Having got that out of the way, let's celebrate what it is that attracts the tourists in their droves. Above us, on its sandstone eminence, is a town of just the right walkable size (population around 5,000), crowned by a sturdy church, with an array of timber-framed, weatherboarded, tile-hung and Georgian-fronted buildings in narrow, often cobbled, streets set inside protecting medieval walls with one surviving gateway. For all its scrabbling for the tourist dollar, Rye seems haughtily independent. From its eastern vantage points it looks out towards the Kent marshes, but is safely withdrawn above them. To the west is the rest of Sussex, but somehow so far away. In my BBC days, charged with spreading the local radio station's output and audience throughout the whole of East Sussex, I attempted to colonise Rye with a missionary zeal, but I always sensed a resistance.

Mermaid Street

The picturesque route to the town centre is up the steep and cobbled incline of Mermaid Street. Take your time, because there are some fine old buildings to enjoy. On the right you'll pass Jeake's House, now a hotel but originally built as a warehouse by Samuel Jeake junior, a devout puritan who nevertheless believed in astrology. High on the wall (though it was shamefully covered in Virginia creeper the last time I passed by) is a plaque with a horoscope detailing the auspicious moment he chose for getting the work under way. A Latin inscription translates into English as: 'At midday on June 13, 1689, the foundation of this warehouse was laid, the heavenly bodies being in these positions.'

The sprawling, timber-framed Mermaid Inn with its first-floor overhang is the pride of the street. The exterior dates from around 1500, but its vaulted cellar was built in the 13th century. Contraband stories are often far-fetched, but there's no doubt that smuggling was rife in Sussex (offering good money at a time when maritime trade and ship-building were in decline) or that the Mermaid was a base for the notorious Hawkhurst Gang. There was, it should be said, little glamour about their activities: they were brutal characters, prepared to maim or kill anyone who got in their way.

The inn is so obviously the chief draw in these parts that the house opposite has been named…well, The House Opposite. It's one of a few jokey monikers here. Lower down there are The House with Two Doors (which it undeniably has) and its neighbour, The House With the Seat (ditto), while at the top of the street, number one would rather be known as The First House.

Lamb House

Just round the corner in West Street is the house built for the 13-times mayor, James Lamb, in 1723. It was here on January 3rd, 1726, that King George I came to stay after taking refuge at Rye during a terrible storm. He was marooned here for several days because of heavy snow-falls and stood as godfather to the Lambs' newborn baby boy – christened George, out of tact if nothing else.

It was here, too, that Allen Grebell – himself mayor for ten years – set off on a foul night in March, 1742, to be murdered by a local butcher, John Breeds. (His skull has been mentioned.) Grebell was the brother-in-law of the then owner, Thomas Lamb, and he made the mistake of borrowing his cloak against the weather. Breeds, who had a grudge against Lamb and was fooled by the cloak, knifed Grebell to death in the churchyard and then ran around the town, presumably drunk, shouting 'Butchers should kill lambs!' His body was hung out on Gibbet Marsh to the south-west of the town. Grebell's grave slab in the church records that he 'fell by the cruel stab of a sanguinary butcher'.

The house, opened by the National Trust twice a week, is best known as the former home of the writer Henry James – he of the labyrinthine expressions of thought and feeling that uncoil like so many wormcasts on the beach. From the narrow Rye perspective, however, an author who rented it within two years of his death is more significant – E.F. Benson, who shared the house with his brother A.C., himself a prolific writer, at one time master of Magdalene College, Cambridge, and the man who penned the words of *Land of Hope and Glory*. Benson wrote the novels set in Rye (thinly disguised as Tilling) which feature the social rivalry of Miss Elizabeth Mapp and Emmeline Lucas, otherwise known as Lucia. These are books full of feline duplicity and wicked one-upmanship – and, fairly or not, we can't help but view cloistered Rye through Benson's eyes. I remember that when approval was given for a plaque honouring the brothers to be affixed to a wall facing the street, the now-defunct Tilling Society refused to pay more than half the cost because their interest was solely in E.F. The self-parody was delicious.

Church Square

Step forward from Lamb House but 100 yards (92 m) and you're in Church Square, a quadrangle of cobbled streets fronted by medieval buildings and, as the name implies, with the church and churchyard at its centre. This is the top of the Rye world and a place to linger.

Look out, on the south side, for the house known as Friars of the Sack. (A previous inhabitant, who was evidently a bit of a showman, used to sit reading in the evening gloom under an atmospheric lamp, with the curtains carefully drawn back: today, I'm afraid, a 'Private' notice warns us against getting too close.) This is the oldest building in the square, dating from the 1260s, and it's made of stone, with gothic arches and decorated tracery. This is no coincidence, because anything constructed of timber was burned to the ground by French raiding parties in the 14th century, when the inhabitants were often put to the sword. It should be added, in fairness, that the favour was often returned. After perhaps the bloodiest incursion, in 1377, the bells of St Mary's Church were carried away across the Channel, this indignity inspiring the men of Rye and Winchelsea to exact revenge the following year and bring them back home.

In the south-east corner of the square is the Ypres Tower, with views across the marshes from the gun garden. It was possibly built as the town's castle as early as the 13th century, although the walls that flank it date from a century later. It became a prison in 1518, has had several other uses over the years and at present houses a museum of local history.

A favourite structure of mine is the unusual oval-shaped brick water cistern just inside the east wall of the churchyard – and, significantly, at the highest point of the town. It has a little cupola on its upper storey, and there's a gauge to show how full it was. Back in the early 18th century the locals had a problem with the water supply, and this was their solution. A horse-powered pump was installed in Cinque Ports Street to raise water to the cistern through a wooden main. A network of pipes and channels then carried it downhill to wherever it was needed.

The church

Look up to the clock (reputed to be the oldest turret clock in Britain with its original works) and you'll see the golden quarterboys poised for action. These cherubs strike the quarter hours but not, to the puzzlement of many an eagerly attentive visitor, the hour itself. Made by Lewys Billiard of Winchelsea in the 1560s, the clock carries a quotation from the *Apocrypha*, rather than the regular biblical cannon: 'For our time is a very shadow that passeth away.' Its 18-ft (5.5-m)-long pendulum swings comfortably in the north transept, and you can see its elaborate workings by climbing the church tower.

E.F. Benson donated the striking west window to the church and dedicated it to his parents, Archbishop and Mrs Benson. He served as mayor on three occasions and is seen in his mayoral robes in the bottom right-hand corner of the window.

The Lookout

The panoramic views from the church tower were doubtless useful in times of trouble, but the Lookout in Watchbell Street (running downhill from the south-west corner of Church Square) was easier for quick access, and a bell was hung here in days gone by to warn of French raids.

The flat area below was once flooded. Indeed, Cadborough Cliff – the higher ground that rises to your right, carries the road to Udimore and forms the landward boundary of Romney Marsh – is an ancient coastline. The sea, as we have seen, is a fickle beast. Some 100,000 years ago, during the last interglacial period, it rose high enough to lap against that cliff face.

A little to our left is Bodiam Castle, while straight ahead, in the middle distance, we can see another stronghold: the almost-island of Winchelsea on its sandstone outcrop.

❷ If you wish to be accepted locally you shouldn't get all fancy with your French, however much it goes against the grain. Remember that the Cinque Ports are pronounced 'sink', while the Ypres Tower (perhaps thanks to tongue-in-cheek British soldiers during World War I) is officially 'Wipers'.

HIGH & DRY

WINCHELSEA TO CLIFF END

Recumbent under ornate ogee-shaped canopies, the ancient effigies in Winchelsea church were once thought to have been carted all the way uphill from the ruins of the old St Thomas before it disappeared under the waves. That would have been a good tale to tell, but the fact that all five date from around 1310-20 – the early years of the new settlement – prompts another train of thought. With what heavy heart did these people set about creating their brave new town, laid out in broad squares in the continental 'bastide' style? How could they not be ever conscious of what they had left behind in the way of hearth and home, of favourite places and, indeed, of memorials such as these to family members they had mourned and seen lowered into graves that were now being carried on their storm-tossed way to far lower depths out at sea?

One of these figures is believed to represent Gervase Alard, Admiral of the Cinque Ports, who died in 1310, and a head that looks down upon him is said to be that of Edward I. This has to be a guess, since the dedications were destroyed at the Reformation, but it makes sense. The King not only ordered the building of the new Winchelsea, but kept a close eye on developments while visiting his friend William of Etchingham at Udimore. Edward was Duke of Gascony, and the trade in wine from the Continent to Sussex was what gave Winchelsea its strategic importance.

The Cellars

On a recent visit to Winchelsea I came across a large pair of wooden shutters pulled back on the pavement to frame a steep flight of stone steps leading down to a dark undercroft. The house, low and white-weatherboarded, dates from around 1700, but what was revealed here was a relic of the New Winchelsea of 700 years ago. A ring of the doorbell, and I was invited to explore for myself. The space was barrel-vaulted with two sturdy stone arches, and here once upon a time, no doubt, was stored some of that Gascony wine.

There are no fewer than 32 accessible medieval vaulted undercrofts in the town – a tally comparable with Southampton, Norwich and Chester – and there must be more under nearby fields where houses once stood. Winchelsea is sufficiently proud of this underground heritage to show it off on an open day each year, but I reckoned that one of them discovered by chance was worth at least a dozen on a guided tour.

Wesley's tree

Outside the western wall of the churchyard is an ash tree descended from the one under which, in October 1790, the great Methodist preacher John Wesley gave his last open-air sermon. In his diary he later lamented the state of the town in words that support the verdict of several other visitors from the late 17th century onwards. He called it 'that poor skeleton of Ancient Winchelsea'.

What on earth had gone wrong?

Ruination

Winchelsea today is a tranquil spot which I swear has its own microclimate: the air seems sweeter, and the late summer flowers seem to bloom here longer than anywhere else. Perhaps this impression derives from the almost unreal serenity of the place. It presents to the visitor a few large squares of amply spaced houses, many of them Georgian, others more recent but in an older style, and all beautifully maintained behind trimmed green verges. The population is around 600, of which half are pensioners and another 20 per cent live here only part of the time. It's so close to a kind of genteel perfection that it comes as a shock to read a Neighbourhood Watch notice outside the post office (open from 9 am to 1.30 pm, Monday to Friday) recording a rise in theft and anti-social behaviour, and adding that 'Indecent behaviour at the public toilets continues to be a problem… Do not tackle suspect characters yourself.' Surely not!

But the manicured village atmosphere of Winchelsea derives from centuries of suffering. The new port was not yet into its stride when the Black Death struck in 1348, in short order killing between a third and a half of the population of southern England. There are no figures for Winchelsea, but we know that closed communities such as monasteries and hospitals were especially vulnerable, and the town had five of these. We also know that by 1358 a third of its properties were uninhabited and in ruins.

This was before the worst of the French raids which, as we have seen at Rye, were ferocious and unpitying. At Winchelsea the insurgents must have found a demoralised people poorly equipped to defend themselves, especially as many of their able-bodied men were serving with the King in France or manning the Cinque Ports ships. Stroll about the streets today and see how little remains. The original plan was for a town of 39 numbered squares: the southern part was never developed, and only 12 are inhabited now.

The church is undeniably grand and spacious when you stand inside it, but what we have now is merely the chancel and its side chapels. It's not clear how much of this cathedral-like building was finished before a declining population made its planned size unrealistic and how much was destroyed by the French. There was another church, St Giles, a little to the south-west, and its last stones were carted away in the 1780s, long after it had been abandoned. (We shall find some of them shortly.) The once substantial St John's Hospital is remembered only by the stark gable end of its chapel, rearing up by the road as you come in from the Hastings end of town. All this makes the survival of the Greyfriars' chancel, in the grounds of a substantial house at the end of Friars Road, something of a miracle: it dates from 1310-20 and is regarded as among the most important Franciscan remains in England.

Three of the four medieval gateways survive. The New Gate (reduced, jackdaw-haunted and way out to the south) is the most atmospheric. The Pipewell is a jagged ruin by the hairpin bend on the main road to Rye. The Strand Gate, which demands great care to drive through, stands above the river which was supposed to give the town its life-blood, but which eventually dwindled virtually to nothing. The sea at last finished off what the plague and the French had already started. Having swamped Old Winchelsea it now washed shingle to the fore-shore and silted up the mouth of the Brede – stranding New Winchelsea and thus bringing it to ruin in its turn.

Winchelsea Beach

Dogs Hill Road, which forks off the coast road from Winchelsea towards the beach, runs past a very long, broad and flat field that stops just short of the high sea wall. Climb the steps and you'll see bulky stones deep in the shingle, forming a large rectangular shape which is extended at a tangent seawards by lines of ancient timbers washed by the tide.

These are the remnants of yet another desperate attempt to defy the elements. During the 1770s, with the old harbour at Rye choked up, it was decided to construct a new one here, and this is all that remains of the eastern pier. If those dimpled, wave-battered stones look rather grand that's not surprising. Up the hill in Winchelsea the splendidly named rector, Drake Hollingberry, wanted to get rid of the ruins of St Giles church, which then stood several feet above the ground. He not only knocked the walls down but had the foundations dug up as well, heartily congratulating himself (in the parish records) for selling the stone to the harbour authorities.

After a great deal of trouble, but clearly without much forethought, the harbour was officially opened in July, 1787. By November its entrance was already blocked by shingle, and so within just a few months the venture came to a shuddering halt. That large green field behind was the harbour basin, and it very soon became filled with silt.

Note that the lower path through Rye Harbour Nature Reserve comes out here. We left it to visit Camber Castle, but in truth it's a much more attractive journey than the bungalow-town drive from Winchelsea. On the large map in the car park at Winchelsea Beach someone has scrawled 'I live here' in indelible ink. Is this a boast or a cry for help?

Defending coastal communities from the sea is an endless task. The Environment Agency has recently spent millions of pounds creating a 2-mile (3.2-km) embankment between Rye Harbour and Winchelsea Beach and constructing concrete and timber 'groyne fields' on the beach between Winchelsea Beach and Cliff End – current thinking prefers 'nourishing' shingle defences rather than erecting solid revetments which will eventually prove powerless in the face of the elements.

The sea wall, made of clay with concrete facing, was erected shortly after the last war and runs westwards for some 3 miles (5 km). You can follow it on foot on the seaward side, where there is good sand and some small rock pools at low tide, or go by road with the ditched marshes of Pett Level on your right. In the middle distance, on high ground south-east of Icklesham, is the black post-mill in which Paul McCartney created a recording studio after he founded Wings.

The Royal Military Canal

Between 1804 and 1809, from Cliff End to Shorncliffe in Kent 28 miles (45 km) away, navvies dug a glorified ditch to deter Napoleon should his troops land on a flat coast that was otherwise protected only by the chain of hastily erected Martello towers. The Royal Military Canal, which 'borrowed' the Brede and the Rother for short stretches, was planned to be 62 ft (19 m) wide and 10 ft (3 m) deep. The end section under the cliff has been built over, and the canal now begins a few yards across the road from the car park as you enter the village.

It was easy to ridicule the canal, and many did so. True, it was useful for moving men and supplies along the line, and it was given slight changes of direction at every 550 yds (500 m) so that cannon could be fired along each stretch, but how would such a narrow waterway foil an enemy which had found the English Channel no great barrier? In the absence of Napoleon, moreover, it offered an enticing passage for contraband. Although soldiers manned guard houses at every bridge across the canal, one of their duties being to catch smugglers, they were apparently easy to bribe. Extra preventative officers had to be employed, paid on a cash-for-prisoner basis.

Today the canal is used by the Environment Agency to manage water levels across the marshes, and it therefore plays a vital role in flood protection. You can walk alongside it back to Winchelsea and then on to Rye, following the long-distance footpath known as the Saxon Shore Way.

A fossilised forest

Walk to the beach, a couple of hundred yards from Pett Level car park, and you'll be treading the remains of a predominantly oak and hazel forest 4,000 years old. The time to come is at low tide. In an outcrop of black peat about 2-ft (60-cm) thick there are well preserved leaves, twigs and branches, with some of the tree boles standing just where they were at the end of the last Ice Age. Neolithic tools have been found here, too. Our travels have already suggested what happened: a rising sea once drowned the forest, but the waters later receded.

Do take care when walking under the cliffs. There is soft clay as well as sand here, and it's easy to sink into it.

● While in the churchyard at Winchelsea look out for the grave of the comedian and former Goon, Spike Milligan, who lived close by at Udimore. Most of the inscription is in English, but the line he insisted on including is given in Gaelic: 'I told you I was ill.'

DOWN THE RUSHY GLENS

HASTINGS COUNTRY PARK

T he foreshore west from Cliff End to Fairlight Cove lies beneath unstable sandstone cliffs which have spilled their detritus onto the beach. The three-toed footprints of a theropod dinosaur have been found here, along with a heady range of fossils – plants, fish scales, shark and crocodile teeth, turtles and iguanodons.

Our route, however, takes us (by foot along the Saxon Shore Way or by road via Fairlight) up high to the 600 acres (240 hectares) of Hastings Country Park. From the cliffs there are views out to the Channel, east to Dungeness and west to Beachy Head. At the Firehills, close to the coastguard station, the heath is a haunt of yellowhammers, stonechats and the rare Dartford warbler, the vegetation a mixture of heather, bracken and the gorse whose deep glow in the season prob-ably gives this stretch its name.

The terrain is easy here, but we're about to undertake the first serious walking of our tour, which will require stout footwear and a strong constitution.

The Wealden anticline

First, though, the most basic of geology lessons from someone certainly unqualified to give anything better. We've travelled the flatlands from Camber to a great hill of sandstone, and we know that the celebrated chalk cliffs of Beachy Head and the Seven Sisters are yet to come. This astounding variety of landscapes in such a relatively small area, creating a comparable variety of vegetation and wildlife, forms the so-called Wealden anticline – and even hard-bitten geologists find it fascinating.

The rocks of Sussex are sedimentary, having been laid down in orderly fashion one on top of the other over millions of years when the land lay beneath shallow lagoons or under the sea. There was sand at the bottom and chalk, in a great dome, at the top. Then came a violent clashing of subterranean tectonic plates, and the landscape fractured and folded.

Now I would ask you to touch the fingers of both hands together. Imagine the forefingers to be the chalk crust and the little fingers to represent the sandstone. Tilt your hands upwards (this is the geological 'uplift') and you'll see that the sandstone rises at the centre. This is Ashdown Forest, while your left and right forefingers are, respectively, the South and the North Downs. The second fingers are the clay of the Low Weald, and the third fingers are the greensand, which at Black Down (just about as far from the coast as you can get) gives us the highest point in Sussex.

Massive erosion and subsequent faulting complicated the picture even further, but what we can plainly see on a geological map of the county is that the chief rocks of Sussex run west to east more or less horizontally. The sandstone of the High Weald meets the sea between Fairlight and Hastings.

Dripping Well

Below the Firehills, stepped footpaths bring us down towards the cliffs, traversing three glens overhung with trees and formed by cascading streams in a landscape fragmented by a jumble of hard stone and soft clay. Warren Glen was, indeed, in medieval times the site of a communal warren providing rabbits for the pot. Fairlight Glen has steps down to the beach, but a notice warns against this potentially hazardous adventure. (When I first knew it some 30 years ago the route was open but I was frustrated in another way. Peregrines, black redstarts and fulmars breed on these cliffs, but my innocent binoculars focused on something altogether different: this was, and remains, a designated nudist beach, which makes life impossible for birders.)

At Ecclesbourne Glen, steps that once led to a former coastguard lookout are now poised in midair, where a 'hanging valley' ends 20 ft (6 m) above the beach.

On a hot day you're immediately plunged into another, far cooler world when you descend under a canopy of sessile oaks, sycamores and beeches, and an underlayer of birch, sallow and alder, to a gurgling sump of running streams and moist vegetation. Dripping Well in Fairlight Glen was a favourite haunt of the Victorians, who loved this evergreen grotto for its faery otherness. Here the rockface, perpetually glistening with water, is thickly matted with moulds, mosses and mildews, while creepers overhang it like a shock of wild, unruly hair. This is a realm of ferns and fungi, sedge and saxifrage.

These glens are known as 'ghyll valleys', and they take us back 8,000 years to when Britain first became an island and had an 'Atlantic' climate. Botanists have found more than 40 mosses and liverworts which survive in only two habitats today: the woodlands of the western coastline from Cornwall to Scotland and the ghylls and damp rock outcrops of the East Sussex sandstone. These otherwise out-of-place species (the ivy-leaved bellflower and the Cornish moneywort are among many more) are believed to be relics of the original flora of lowland Britain which have clung to life in this special microclimate.

Covehurst Wood

On the cracked and unstable undercliff south-west of Fairlight Glen is a forest of hunched and stunted oaks and willows, bent away from the prevailing Channel winds. Here's another magical place where you can leave the world behind. Whitethroats, chiffchaffs and nightingales inhabit the tangled hawthorn and dogwood scrub, bush crickets hide in cracks in the rock and great crested newts swim in iron-rich ponds the colour of rust. Above you, flying off a cliff face covered in cushions of thrift, are gulls, cormorants, kestrels and jackdaws.

This is good fossil-hunting territory. I well remember returning from an outing here with a collector and accidentally spilling a find on to one of my children's supper plates. It was difficult to persuade him that the little dry lump was harmless since I had already proudly trumpeted the fact that it was nothing less than dinosaur dung.

The East Hill

Emerging from Ecclesbourne Glen you climb to a wide, green area with thickets of gorse and blackthorn. This is the East Hill, a scheduled ancient monument because of the iron age fort whose embankments can still be seen. Evidence of later Romano-British and Saxon settlers has also been found, and there was once a windmill here, too.

Keep to the cliff path and you eventually look down on Hastings. You can lumber down a flight of 272 steps to the foot of the hill or have yourself deposited there by the vertiginous East Cliff Railway, the steepest funicular in the country – it was water-powered when it opened in 1902.

❷ A mystery on the hilltop before you descend. The raised, rectangular outline of 'St George's churchyard' is marked out in the turf. The name is first mentioned in 1291 – but unfortunately there's no evidence that a church ever stood here.

FRESH FISH & RAGGED TROUSERS

HASTINGS

This is where to begin in Hastings – down on the shingle at the Stade, between the tarred wooden winch huts, among faded old boats draped with cloths, heaps of discarded paraphernalia (rusted wire cages, lengths of cable, old paint cans), lobster pots piled high like modernist sculptures, collections of fibreglass buoys sporting black polythene flags atop their poles, rusted caterpillar tractors with large rubber tyres lashed to the front.

'A Working Beach Has Hazards' read the signs, and you certainly shouldn't get under their boots while the men are hauling the boats ashore. Each vessel has its own slipway, marked less obviously by the wire uncoiled from the winches at the top of the beach (and operated by so-called 'boys ashore') than by the flotsam and jetsam of working life that lie alongside to right and left – that rubbish, those buoys and lobster pots, with just the occasional frond of sea kale waving forlornly in the salt breeze.

A pebble's throw away is a tourist information centre and parking for luxury coaches, and closer still are the famous 'net shops' – tall, black, wooden storage sheds, first built here centuries ago which have been renovated by the Old Hastings Preservation Society, Hastings Borough Council and English Heritage, and attract photographers who bang off souvenir pictures at almost any time of the day and night.

But as one of the corroded tractors sputters into life, ready to swivel down a runway and push a boat into the sea, you realise that all this 'heritage' is a world away. We're in working Hastings here, and the rust is a badge of honour. The fishermen are proud to own the largest beach-launched fleet in Britain, and there's a don't-give-a-damn tinge to their pride. Their cussed, beleaguered history testifies to it – their independence and their ownership of the foreshore has been a long-running battle – and the website of the Fishermen's Protection Society keeps the pot simmering:

> Hastings Council has continued to pursue its aggressive, short-sighted and damaging policies. This unfortunate hostility from Hastings Council provides the ever-present backdrop to fishing on the Stade, and no more so than since the end of the Second World War.

Down at heel

There's a definite edge to Hastings, and the friction between the fishermen and the authorities is only a part of it. The truth is that ever since its first flush of success as a resort the place seems to have been giving itself a wash and brush-up without quite managing to appear respectable. Robert Tressell, who died in 1914, set *The Ragged Trousered Philanthropists* here, its 'heroes' a group of oppressed labourers exploited by their bosses and corrupt politicians. After the last war the town accommodated large numbers of poorer families from London, many of them living on benefits: some, of course, later prospered, but the law of averages has bestowed a legacy of ragged trousered deprivation. Handsome houses here go for a (relative) song. Most seaside towns of any size have clusters of quality hotels – here there isn't a single one.

In the 30 years that I've known Hastings the bootstraps have been pulled time and again, but the poor old creature still has a bent back. The latest wheeze to brighten it up involves a 'grotbusters' team sent in by the planners to threaten the owners of dilapidated properties with a £1,000 fine plus £100 each day thereafter until everything is spick and span. The seafront was certainly stacked with more scaffolding than I can remember the last time I visited, but experience counsels a large dollop of scepticism.

And yet – buy fresh fish from the little huts in the fishermen's quarter, look up from the Stade to the tawny, honeycombed sandstone cliffs, taste some of the best fish and chips of your life in the unpretentious restaurants around Winkle Island (where the coast road, the Bourne, turns sharply north towards Rye) and you'll surely feel that Hastings is by far the most invigorating seaside resort in Sussex. Even the gulls seem to call more raucously here.

The sea, the sea!

In short, Hastings simply has more of the sea about it than anywhere else. The catch is auctioned at the fishmarket on the Stade early in the morning, while above the large market hall are the offices of the Fishermen's Protection Society and the government's South East Fisheries inspector (not to speak of an excellent fish café). Walk along the short road called Rock-a-Nore, under the East Cliff, and you pass whelk and cockle stalls, a fishing museum in the former fisher-men's church, the Underwater World attraction and the Shipwreck and Coastal Heritage Centre on your way to the local motor boat and yacht club. Retrace your steps and you come across the coastguard station, the lifeboat station and the headquarters of the East Hastings Sea Angling Association.

The natural harbour became silted up centuries ago, but the break-water to the east of the fishermen's beach is the last remnant of a 19th-century attempt to create a new one, and a testimony to the dogged determination of the locals to earn a living from the waves.

At Brighton the sea is an enticing add-on for jaded and sophisticated palates – at Hastings everything derives from it.

The Old Town

Lying between the East and West cliffs, on either side of the Bourne Valley, are the secretive twittens, the steep steps and the huddled, clustered shops and houses of Hastings Old Town. (These gems are easily missed if you find yourself seduced by the largely pedestrianised modern shopping centre further to the west.) From Rock-a-Nore you climb All Saints Street with, eventually, All Saints Church off to your right. This was always the poorer end of town, inhabited by fishing families, although today the timber-framed buildings are immaculately kept. Look out, at the bottom of the street, for the 'Piece of Cheese' – a house tucked into a wedge-shaped corner of land and, fittingly, painted yellow.

The better-off lived to the west of the valley, in High Street and the passages climbing from it into the hillside. Here there are more handsome timber-framed houses, while the most notable feature of street is the raised pavement on its western side. The parish church is St Clement, which originally stood further down but was threatened by regular incursions of the sea during the 13th century: those who enjoy somewhat laboured coincidences may like to know that it, too, has been fitted into an awkwardly shaped piece of land – donated in 1286 by Alan the Cheesemonger.

George Street, closed to traffic and touristy ('A tarot reader's *just* the kind of thing we need here,' gushed someone in the Village Arcade as I passed), runs west from near the foot of High Street to meet the seafront. The West Hill lift, far less steep than its cousin to the east, offers a painless way up to the castle through a rocky cleft.

The castle & caves

After 1066, William the Conqueror divided Sussex into five (later six) administrative 'rapes', each with a port, a castle and a productive hinterland. Not only was the castle at Hastings built on a cliff, but an impressive ditch was carved through the rock to make its 11 acres (4.5 hectares) an island site. What we see today are the remains of about half of it, the rest crumbled into the sea during the same period that Winchelsea was inundated.

The caves in the West Hill have, inevitably, become an 'experience' known as Smugglers Adventure, although there's no evidence that contraband was ever stowed here – it would have been a bit of a climb with a full barrel, even if you were rolling it. But an eye for the tourist shilling isn't new: Joseph Golding, a local grocer, first developed the caves into an attraction during the 19th century, creating a ball-room and other facilities and, in 1864, welcoming the Prince and Princess of Wales to his establishment.

Little enlarge

It would be unkind to say that what the Prince Regent was to Brighton, so Sidney Little, 'the concrete king', was to Hastings. The town had, of course, been developed long before he was appointed borough engineer in 1926 and then, in 1945, town planning and development officer as well – and, for the record, we should credit John Collier for the town's earliest period of seaside prosperity in the first half of the 18th century. But Mr Little, champion of a 'bold and courageous' reordering of the townscape (knocking down buildings and obliterating ancient streets to create a better traffic flow, for instance), keeps coming to mind as we leave the fishermen's quarter and head west on foot towards St Leonards.

First, the amusements – the helter skelter, ghost train, go karts, crazy golf, candy floss 'n' donuts, all the flagrant kiss-me-quickery that disfigures the eastern seafront. The fishermen felt that they had been horribly dumped upon, and it's hard to disagree with them, although one has to ask whether Hastings would be the vigorous place it is without the tat.

Soon we come to the shallow boating lake dug in 1933 to give men employment, and a little further on we reach what are claimed to be the world's first underground car parks. (They are, of course, made of concrete.) And then Little's pride and joy, the half-mile covered promenade from the pier to Warrior Square, its inner wall studded with roundels of broken glass, so earning it the soubriquet Bottle Alley: enthusiasts spend happy hours discovering the relics of former breweries and their tipples. Gone now are the glazed shutters that once slid across against the weather, and rust is breaking through.

Below par

Nikolaus Pevsner describes the White Rock Pavilion as being 'in the Spanish Mission style of America', which is useful for those of us pondering what kind of pastiche it can be, and it's certainly sprucely kept. Unfortunately there's very little else to catch the eye along the front.

Pelham Crescent, built for the Earl of Chichester in the 1820s, is a shot at Georgian elegance that doesn't quite come off. At its centre is St Mary-in-the-Castle Church, which is built into the West Hill below the castle. Pevsner thinks the overall design fails because the houses are too tall, but I'd point the finger at the ghastly arches underneath, with their chipped paint of different colours and their garish signage (amusements, humbugs, more fish 'n' chips) that distracts the eye from the elegance beyond. Only in Hastings...

And then the wretched pier, designed by the great Eugenius Birch, modelled on Brighton's slightly earlier West Pier, and opened with pomp and ceremony on the country's first ever bank holiday – August 5th, 1872. A rash of small buildings was planted on it early in the 20th century, completely ruining its design, and the original oriental-style pavilion at the seaward end was replaced by something much more mundane after it was destroyed by fire in 1917. This is the first pier we have met on our travels and it's in such a sorry state of disrepair that only the front of it is open – and that for a bar, amusements and 'De Luxe Gaming'. Throwing small change away on fruitless pursuits is an integral part of pier enjoyment, but it's nothing if not combined with a walk over the water.

It's a relief, finally, to take the steps down from the promenade to a board which alerts you to what you might see passing at different times of the year: harbour porpoises, bottlenose dolphins, long-finned pilot whales. Ah, that's better – Hastings and the sea!

◗ A hidden secret of Hastings, although it's all of 2^1/$_2$ miles (4 km) from top to bottom, is Alexandra Park. It runs down from a nature reserve in a wooded valley at the top to manicured parkland with a vast collection of trees as it descends to the town centre just above the railway line. Its other attractions range from a bandstand and a bowling green to a boating lake.

A DEVELOPER'S DREAM

BURTON'S ST LEONARDS

One night during the 1820s the builder James Burton, already responsible for substantial developments in the heart of London, had a dream in which he created a beautiful new 'Regent's Park by the sea'. That, at any rate, is the story, although it wouldn't have taken much waking imagination to recognise that the lucrative flowering of Brighton was ripe for replication a little further along the coast. St Leonards would become the first purpose-built resort of the new tourist age.

The spot Burton chose then lay 2 miles (3.2 km) west of Hastings where, below the cliffs, a small ravine ran down to the sea. The approach from the east today suggests a complete merging of the two towns – Marine Court, a 1930s 13-storey ocean liner of a building with rust and decay at its shop-front level, is hardly welcoming – but much of Burton's St Leonards can still be discovered.

Work began in 1828 (Burton's architect son Decimus, although originally doubtful about the enterprise, was to complete it in 1877), and the very first building to be erected can still be seen on the front at number 57 Marina. Timber-framed and collonaded, this was Burton's own house, made at his London workshop and transported in sections by sea. In 1834 he generously (please don't be cynical) put it at the disposal of the young Princess Victoria, who enjoyed a winter holiday in the budding resort and helped put it on the map. It was swiftly named Victoria House, and then Crown House when Victoria became queen.

Two terraces of stuccoed brick with Tuscan and Ionic columns flank the seaward entrance to Burton's new town. The major building was the hydro – soon renamed the Royal Victoria Hotel – and behind it were the assembly rooms (Doric columns), now the masonic hall.

Seaside architecture

Spotting the architectural influences is an entertaining game to play here. In East Ascent, for instance, there's a distinct echo of some of Burton's Bloomsbury terraces. Further up, in the streets which surround St Leonards Gardens (landscaped in a former quarry and originally exclusive to families who paid a subscription), you'll find a gloriously confident mishmash of Greek, Roman, English medieval and Scottish baronial styles.

The way into the new town from the landward end was beneath the castellated North Lodge. In the years after World War I the novelist Sir Henry Rider Haggard, author of *She* and *King Solomon's Mines*, lived here. Allegria Court, near the top of Quarry Hill, became James Burton's home in his later years: the entrance arch he had driven through a sandstone outcrop still survives, but it's badly weathered now.

To the east of the central area lie two mini-suburbs created by Burton. Mercatoria was the shopping district, designed to cater for the working classes. A National School was built here in 1847 and now houses the Masjid Al-Haq mosque for a local Muslim population of around 600 people. Nearby is Lavatoria, the laundry area, where some of Burton's original cottages can still be seen.

The original church, west along the seafront, was destroyed by a flying bomb in 1944. Sir Giles and Adrian Gilbert Scott designed a Gothic brick replacement in the 1950s.

❯ The Burton family graveyard, approached along West Hill Road, is on high ground overlooking the sea. The developer and his wife died within months of each other in 1837, and they lie in a vault with a pyramidal top – family tradition asks us to believe that this was to avoid the eastern curse: 'May jackasses sit on your grandfather's grave'.

EDWARDIAN SLUMBER

BULVERHYTHE TO BEXHILL

West of St Leonards the land is flat, for we have almost (but not quite) done with the sandstone. To the north is the Combe Haven valley, a world of pools and ditches, reeds and fen, scrub and woodland – a vulnerable nature reserve through which a new Bexhill to Hastings link road is to be carved. This will be a second scarring of the landscape: the present route inland to the garish retail 'park' at Glyne Gap is so hideous that the passing motorist easily forgets that there is a world of sea, shingle and low cliffs behind the buildings and the railway line. In fact a broad, firm path on the landward side of the sea defences – massive granite rocks at the eastern end – makes for easy walking all the way to Bexhill.

The wreck of the Amsterdam

Visit Bulverhythe at a very low tide if you can, with turnstones and, in winter, purple sandpipers feeding among the intertidal rocks. When the lowest sandstone bed is exposed you can see dinosaur footprints, a stretch of petrified Bronze Age forest and the outline of a ship which sank here, in dramatic circumstances, in January 1749. (There's an information board near the railway footbridge from the A259.) This was the *Amsterdam*, a three-masted Dutch East Indiaman whose crew were struck down by yellow fever soon after sailing out of Rotterdam for Java with a cargo of silver, cloth and wine. Fifty men were dead and

40 ill by the time she reached this part of the Channel; her rudder was damaged in a violent storm, and the surviving sailors mutinied and broke open the wine bottles to give themselves (literal) Dutch courage as she drifted ashore. Although the mayor had the silver promptly removed to the customs house under guard, the *Amsterdam* was callously looted even as members of her crew lay dying. Today she's a protected wreck.

Galley Hill

The soft, sandy outcrops a little further on towards Bexhill are so low and worn that the 'Beware falling rocks' sign at first seems a little over-protective – until, that is, you see the sizeable boulders dotted about the path and spot the deep cracks which show where the next crumbling will occur. The concrete footings of a long-abandoned structure were precariously poised at the top of a bluff the last time I visited, and they will almost certainly have come crashing down by now.

Galley Hill is much more substantial than this, although it, too, is being worn away. It once sported its own Martello tower, but that has long since been undermined and washed out to sea. There was an Admiralty signalling station here from the late 18th century, and this ages-old use of the hilltop was commemorated in 2005 by the erection of an iron cresset next to the little whitewashed coastguard house.

Just to the west of the hill is a marker showing the finishing line of the motor racing track which once, and briefly, ran along the eastern end of Bexhill seafront.

Bexhill-on-Sea

There have been various attempts to enliven Bexhill, but it really wants to be left alone if you don't very much mind. In 1804, when it was but a village on a hill, more than 3,000 men of the King's German Legion breezed in to defend the area against Napoleon, building a huge barracks, laying out a parade ground and generally doing what soldiers do – including marrying many of the local girls. They left ten years later to fight in the Battle of Waterloo, and the metaphorical curtains were promptly snatched back into place again: *Black's Guide to Sussex* of 1861 (some 15 years after the railway had arrived close by) recorded a population of just over 2,000.

During the 1880s, which was somewhat late in the day, the De La Warr family decided to embrace the resorts craze. The seventh Earl erected a sea wall, developed broad parades on what had been marshy ground, built the Sackville Hotel (now apartments) and gave the place its 'On Sea' tag. Sturdy, dutch-gabled terraces of hotels and boarding houses set the tone. Boarding schools swarmed at the new resort, catering in large part for the children of parents serving the British Empire overseas.

The eighth Earl was even more energetic, and the Edwardian period was Bexhill's heyday. He moved the railway station closer to the centre and built an entertainments pavilion, the Kursaal, on the seafront – it was demolished in 1936. In 1901 Bexhill became the first resort in the country to sanction mixed bathing. A year later a cycle track created at the eastern end of De la Warr Parade became the course for the first motor race in Britain, when the 200 competitors included Alfred Harmsworth, later Lord Northcliffe, who had recently founded the *Daily Mail*. The event would have been repeated, but a local resident took out an injunction preventing it, while the opening of the purpose-built Brooklands circuit in Surrey meant that (although Bexhill's tourism department still trades on it) the excitement was short-lived. The Earl, twice sued for divorce, eventually ran out of money.

That thankfully (*see page 44*) wasn't quite the end of the De la Warr influence, but the town must have been glad to be done with all the excitement. The independent schools were evacuated during World War II and closed soon afterwards, while tourists found more exciting places to spend their time and money. Bexhill's 'unique selling point' today is having the oldest population in western Europe. Walk around the streets in the centre and you sense something strange in the atmosphere. It's the quiet: there are cars, of course (although surely no local would think of sounding the horn), but they glide quietly by while elderly shoppers talk almost in whispers. The street signs are discreet and sometimes missing, as if nobody from outside were ever expected to intrude. But this isn't God's proverbial waiting room: the inhabitants display not a fearful apprehension of mortality but an enviable, placid contentment.

The De la Warr Pavilion

What a strange place, therefore, to find such a Modernist landmark as the De La Warr Pavilion, which presents a bold sweep of glass-and-concrete terraces to the sea. It was promoted by the ninth Earl, who had become the town's first socialist mayor and successfully argued that it should be financed from public funds to give 'that pleasure, that culture which hitherto the gloom and dreariness of British resorts have driven our fellow countrymen to seek in foreign lands'. More than 200 architects entered a competition for the design, the winners being Erich Mendelsohn (at one time more famous than Le Corbusier and Mies van der Rohe) and Serge Chermayeff. It opened in 1935.

Inevitably, many of the locals grumbled about the design and the cost, and the Earl was sufficiently upset by the fuss to turn down a proffered freedom of the borough. Although the building has suffered long periods of neglect, however, a recent £8 million refurbishment has restored its clean lines and its wonderful airiness. It contains an art gallery and an auditorium, and – especially when the sky is blue – is a great place for lunch.

The Old Town

It's a climb of a good half mile (0.8 km) from the front to the original part of Bexhill, where St Peter's Church is flanked by a group of old buildings, including a 15th-century Wealden house. The nearby manor house was pulled down to widen the road in the unforgiving 1960s, but its barn survives and its footings provide secluded pockets in what has become an ornamental public garden.

❯ Church 'sitters' at St Peter's Church are on duty only at lunchtimes during the week, but do look out for 'the Bexhill stone' if you manage to get in. Discovered under the nave floor, and possibly placed in the original church here more than 1,200 years ago, it's thought to be the lid of a reliquary – a container for the relics of a saint. The elaborate carving is Celtic in design, and the stone is of a type found only in the north of England.

ON THE LEVEL

APPROACHES TO PEVENSEY

Beyond Cooden the flatlands of the Low Weald sweep down to the sea – an extensive patchwork of unkempt fields set among a grid of reed-lined, willow-flanked drainage ditches. The spare landscape of the Pevensey Levels is home to an astonishing array of wildlife: some 70 per cent of all the aquatic plant species found in Britain, more than 100 kinds of rare insects, 21 different dragonflies, water voles, marsh frogs madly cackling in the spring, huge (but harmless) fen raft spiders and blood-sucking leeches which, from their home in the ooze, fasten upon a plentiful supply of fish and other prey. Noctule and serotine bats flit overhead on autumn evenings, feeding on the dung beetles around the grazing cattle, while the ornithologist is entertained throughout the year by a constant parade of resident birds, migrants and flocking winter visitors.

Beneath the grassy tussocks on a bed of impervious clay is a slew of shingle, sand, mud, peat, the alluvium of centuries. Intertidal mudflats long ago gave way to salt marsh – the Saxons created pans for evaporating water to get salt, and these survive as low mounds some 40 ft (12 m) wide – and then to today's freshwater marsh behind a protecting shingle bank, the best site in Britain for freshwater molluscs.

Crooked Ditch on Hooe Level was a 14th-century sea defence. Much of the area was under water when the Normans arrived an arrow's flight from here in 1066, and successive generations – among them the monks of Battle Abbey – attempted to reclaim the land for agriculture. A map reveals that this struggle was often unavailing: the medieval settlement at Northeye has been swallowed (the 'eye' suffixes in the area signify an island in the water meadows), while the site of Manxey village is marked only by the remains of its moat.

The dykes have long been sluiced and pumped, but a large area around Pevensey Bridge Level is a national nature reserve and has a special drainage regime to preserve its precious diversity of flora and fauna – the road from Normans Bay to Pevensey crosses it. These levels have a raw and haunting beauty, to which the fringing bungalow and caravan park developments, running in a narrow strip along the coast, offer a loud and brazen raspberry.

Costa del Shingle

People must take their pleasures as they can, but to witness this brave colonisation of bare shingle (with, granted, a ribbon of sand along the foreshore when the tide is out) is to understand why Spanish resorts do such good business. Could there really be a nudist beach at Normans Bay? Indeed there is, and has been unofficially for some 30 years – although one recent contributor to a naturists' website found sharing the pebbles with clothed rod fishermen a little offputting.

After Normans Bay, with a former coastguard house (good smuggling terrain) and a Martello tower, we reach first the Beachlands estate – the shabby, bungaloid relic of a 1930s attempt at something grand, with a boulevard and a square – and then the 'capital' of this something-out-of-nothing stretch of coast, Pevensey Bay.

This is a larger Camber Sands, without the sand or the holiday camp but with a little more money to spend. The truncated promenade is potholed, but the houses behind it are jauntily verandahed, the cars parked on it include some gleaming 4x4s and the varnished yachts hauled up in front of it (there's also a sailing club to the west) speak of leisurely g&ts rather than broiling seas.

Along the main road to Eastbourne (launderette, betting shop, fast food outlets) we find hints that there may be something even better than this English holiday heaven. One of the estate agents is given over entirely to selling flats at Sovereign Harbour, the newly created marina on the Crumbles just along the coast at Eastbourne, while a huge banner on the Baptist church urges us to 'Explore the meaning of life' through an Alpha course. Unfortunately, the line 'For details contact…' has been left unfinished, so we shall have to carry our windbreaks gingerly over the unforgiving shingle without knowing quite why we do it.

Pevensey & the castle

Faded glory is better than none at all, and Pevensey is the attractive remnant of a once-flourishing port town. (It lost its borough status as recently as 1886.) The gabled, oak-beamed, 14th-century Old Mint House in the main street is, indeed, on the site of the former Norman mint, while the Court House, with a council chamber upstairs and a prison below, is claimed to be the smallest town hall in England.

What gave the place its distinction was the castle, built on a natural mound during the Roman occupation of Sussex, when the sea lapped at its feet. The massive brick and flint bastions, outer walls and gateways were built around AD 290 to keep land-hungry Saxons at bay – something they failed to do after the legions withdrew and the Romano-British Celts had to fend for themselves. The Saxon leader Aelle overran the castle in 491, killing everyone inside it.

The castle thereafter suffered nearly six centuries of neglect until the Conquest. The Normans dug a moat, repaired the walls and built their own stone keep, gatehouse and other defences within them. It survived various sieges over the years and was used as a gaol during the 15th century: a deep pit just inside the entrance was an *oubliette* into which prisoners were dropped – and, as the name implies, effectively forgotten.

Look out, too, for the mound where a gun emplacement was thrown up in the outer bailey at the time of the Spanish Armada, and for artfully disguised machine-gun posts dating from World War II.

❯ A note for birders: the village of Wartling, north across the levels from Pevensey, has several heronries close to the church, whose lectern, fittingly, is a heron rather than the traditional eagle.

BUILT FOR GENTLEMEN

EASTBOURNE

W hat would the 7th Duke of Devonshire have made of Sovereign Harbour? He it was who, having become one of the wealthiest men in the land when he inherited the title in 1858, set about creating the spacious resort of Eastbourne at which we shall soon arrive.

In his day the Crumbles was a broad shingle waste to the east, watched over by a string of Martello towers, and so it was to remain until the close of the 20th century – with a flurry of unwanted fame in the 1920s when two grisly murders were committed here. Now it's become the largest marina of its kind in Europe, with thousands of houses and apartments grouped skilfully around large yacht basins.

The Duke's watering place was described as being 'built *by* gentlemen *for* gentlemen,' and I suspect that he would have approved not only of the entrepreneurial flair on display here but of the clientele, too: after all, anyone who can afford to live in one of the waterside penthouses with private pontoons is probably the nearest thing we have to a gentleman of the Victorian age.

There's money and not a little pretension here. I stole inside from the beach close to one of the Martello towers and found myself in a 'private' quarter comprising Callao Quay, Arequipa Reef and (doubtful associations, perhaps) Trujillo Court, in which a vigorous fountain played over glistening rocks. There are many such wealthy pockets here, some securely gated, with names redolent of the high seas and safe havens in exotic spots around the world. They have 'private beaches', too, although it's not obvious to the passer-by which patches of shingle are exclusive to the owners unless it be the small sections railed off at the foot of the buildings.

But it's an unattractive trait to sneer at other people's pleasures. The harbour may lack high culture and even a few of the lowlier creature comforts (one resident told me that the only thing he missed was a corner shop – an amusing notion in these surroundings), but there are shops, bars and restaurants and always, even for those in the cheaper houses, the proximity of the sea. Those who like this kind of thing will like it very much indeed.

The Redoubt

Rounding Langney Point we fairly soon come to a low circular fortress built in Napoleonic times to supplement the firepower of the Martello towers. The Redoubt has 24 casemates, or barrack rooms, around a central parade ground, and originally pointed ten cannons out to sea: they fired only two shots in anger, in 1815, and both missed their French target. Once that threat had passed the fort fell into disuse, although it became an observation post during World War I and housed Canadian troops in World War II, when a battery of anti-aircraft guns was mounted on top.

Today it contains a museum which traces the history of the armed forces in Sussex over the centuries and displays the collections of the Royal Sussex Regiment and the Queen's Royal Irish Hussars.

Eastbourne pier

And then it's on to the first accessible pier of our journey – an 1870s confection neatly done out in blue and white, with a pavilion and fetching little cupolas. Apart from the usual slot machines, bars, restaurants and nightclub, there's a glass-blowing studio, a pier angling club (non-members £2 a rod) and, in a dome near the seaward end, a camera obscura, its Victorian projector capturing the views for 360 degrees around.

But you can take in a magnificent view from the end of the pier in any case. To the east you have the sandstone cliffs beyond Hastings; to the west the Downs rise up from the sea; while directly inland are the Duke's broad and terraced parades with their backdrop of imposing hotels.

In keeping with the desired gentility of the place, the use of deck chairs on the pier is free; you are thoughtfully told that 'it is advisable to hold handrail when windy'; while potentially rowdy gangs of revellers are (perhaps) lulled by a terribly polite notice above the exit: 'The management respectfully request that patrons leaving the pier at night do so quietly. Thank you.'

In defence of dullness

And what's wrong with a little gentility? Look, it's easy to point the finger at Eastbourne's dullness, its manicured carpet gardens and its let's-pretend-this-is-the-Mediterranean palms, yuccas and gingers. The common belief is that it's a haunt of the elderly – and the guesthouses and hotels certainly attract the white-haired in droves – but you're more likely to be mown down by roller skates than invalid carriages as you stroll along the prom.

Inland, the town has spread formlessly. A little back from the front it retains some grandeur, with wide avenues, greenery and bow-fronted terraces, but otherwise it's just a typical modern mish-mash. The verdant and capacious seafront is its glory, and among the Duke's legacies is the absence of anything commercial close to the beach – unless, of course, you count the boat trips, the occasional ice cream kiosk and the track-less Dotto train. (This carries advertising boards and was criticised for lowering the tone when it was introduced in the 1970s.)

Where around Winkle Island in Hastings you have humble shellfish stalls and cheap chippies, here you have the Café Belge ('50 ways to eat mussels') facing a branch of Harry Ramsden's across the top of Terminus Road. While Hastings has a fishing museum, a top Eastbourne attraction is the How We Lived Then celebration of shopping and social history. The Hastings seafront is heavily scaffolded, whereas Eastbourne's always seems freshly painted without a hint of intrusive human agency.

And yes, you feel you should perhaps brush your shoes on the mat before stepping into Eastbourne, whereas you'd give them a good wipe on coming *out* of Hastings – but few of us wish to spend our lives metaphorically always in the leather armchair of the club or on the high stool of the public bar. We need both.

The bandstand & beyond

Eastbourne was the first British seaside resort to have its own orchestra. A plaque on a wall of the impressive 1930s bandstand (which replaced a prettier but much smaller 'birdcage' structure) honours one of its regulars, John Wesley Woodward, who was lost in April 1912 while a member of the ship's orchestra on the *Titanic*.

On Wednesday nights during the season visiting military bands perform the 1812 overture as fireworks light up the sky.

Further along, beyond a restrained row of beach huts, are the lifeboat museum and the Wish Tower – a Martello tower-cum-puppet museum. You'll find little iron plates affixed to the wall by the road here, bearing letters such as BCS, SPS and HCS: bath chair stand, saddled pony stand and hackney carriage stand respectively, with others for motor charabancs, saddled donkeys and goat chaises.

Eventually we reach the wide western lawns with the five-star Grand Hotel set behind. The BBC Palm Court Orchestra (but of course) used to broadcast regularly from its Great Hall.

It was to the Grand that the composer Debussy scandalously fled from France in the summer of 1905 with his pregnant mistress, completing the orchestration of *La Mer* while he was here.

'The sea displays herself with a strictly British correctness,' he wrote to a friend, later describing Eastbourne as 'a little English seaside town, as ridiculous as these sorts of places always are'.

But nobody asked him to come.

❯ At the far end of the seafront is Holywell, where the land falls away to the sequestered Italian Gardens in a former chalkpit. The second in the row of beach huts further down bears a surprising plaque: 'This chalet was used by Their Majesties King George V and Queen Mary in the month of March, 1935.'

THYME & VETCH

BEACHY HEAD TO SEAFORD HEAD

N ow we climb the steep hill from the western corner of Eastbourne and enter an invigorating new world of fresh breezes, springy turf and the skylark's song. The Victorian nature writer Richard Jefferies called it 'the land of health'. We've arrived at the chalk, and the Downs will be with us for the rest of our journey – at first close to the sea and under our feet, as here, and then as a green, inviting backdrop inland.

It is, too, the land of flint. The chalk accumulated at the rate of about a foot every 30,000 years over some 30 million years, and at various periods nodules of silica hardened on the sea bed to form broad bands of a material far harder than the white deposits in which it lay. While neolithic people sunk hundreds of mines to find flints for their tools and weapons, modern man has made use of the plentiful supply littering the fields and foreshore to create boundary walls, dove-cotes, barns and houses which are a distinguishing feature of our downland landscape.

It doesn't take much imagination to hear ancestral voices all about us. Mesolithic hunter-gatherers left dozens of axes at Bullock Down, and the map is sprinkled with the tumuli, trackways, hill-forts and field systems of their successors, who hacked away the original tree cover to create productive corn-and-sheep farms on what, by the Iron Age, had become a densely inhabited landscape. When farms moved down to villages under 'the hill' in medieval times, the Downs were given over to sheep pasture – as they were until the last war when arable agriculture climbed the slopes. Now most of the sheep have gone, and scrub invades areas that have been spared the plough.

The chalk is covered with a thin layer of poor 'rendzina' soil, unsuitable for high-yielding crops without the introduction of fertilisers, but allowing the spread of violets, harebells, orchids, cowslips and sweet-smelling herbs such as marjoram, basil and wild thyme. At one time the sheep-cropped turf was among the richest wildlife habitats in western Europe – carpeted with as many as 40 different flower species per square yard, attracting swarms of butterflies and alive with bees, grasshoppers, glow-worms and chalk-loving snails – but very little remains as it was.

That said, and lamented, it's a joy to stride out on the roof of the world, looking down upon white-capped waves to one side and the wooded Weald to the other. The South Downs Way starts here and finishes more than 100 miles (160 km) away in Hampshire: we're about to walk one of the finest stretches of it, a leg-testing, up-and-down march of 10 miles (16 km) or so over the top of the Seven Sisters.

Beachy Head

The cliffs of Dover may have a whiteness immortalised in song, but they are certainly *not* as gleaming as the magnificent chalk stacks which front the sea between Eastbourne and Seaford.

Beachy Head (the Normans' 'beau chef', or beautiful headland) is the highest point on the south coast at 534 ft (163 m), and has its own sad fame, albeit not yet set to music, as a lure for would-be suicides. From above you look vertiginously down to the red-and-white lighthouse built, with great ingenuity and daring, in 1902 – a 600-ft (183-m) aerial tramway carried men and supplies from a high point on the cliff down to the large construction platform far below.

A footpath takes you down to the beach at Cow Gap, where the geological strata are laid bare: gault clay at the foot, upper greensand above it and then the great mass of the chalk, comprising various marls and limestones. Some bands are rich in fossils, including ammonites and sponges, and the tiny holes you see are caused by the tunnel burrowing of a marine worm.

At low tide there are plenty of rock pools to explore between here and Birling Gap, but be aware that 'escape routes' under the cliffs are few, and that you therefore need to check the tide times before wandering far from one.

Fulmars, herring gulls and kittiwakes are among the many birds which nest on the narrow ledges above your head, and if you see a speeding falcon effortlessly snatch a jackdaw or a feral pigeon it will be one of the peregrines which have returned to Sussex in recent years after a period of local extinction. Another recent returnee to excite ornithologists here is the raven.

Belle Tout

The cliffs are crumbling at the rate of about 3 ft (1 m) a year, with occasional dramatic falls to intensify the unease of anyone living literally near the edge. It's therefore remarkable that the owners of the former lighthouse on the downland just to the west of Beachy Head should have thought it worthwhile to have their home physically moved away from danger.

But so it was. In March 1999, with the garden patio by now only three yards from the precipice – and watched by TV crews, reporters and a large crowd who had bought tickets for the event – engineers delicately winched Belle Tout 55 ft (17 m) down the slope. That's still pretty close to the drop for anyone who suffers from vertigo, but the new foundation of concrete and steel which underlies the building allows for another hydraulically powered trundling when the need arises again. At the time of writing, Belle Tout was up for sale.

Built at the vigorous instigation of John 'Mad Jack' Fuller, the wealthy and eccentric MP for Sussex at the time, she is a jaunty little structure but was never much cop as a lighthouse. Her oil lamps, first lit in 1834, were visible 23 miles (37 km) out to sea in good weather, but the clifftop was so often smothered in fog that she was decommissioned in 1902 and replaced by the current Beachy Head light, which stands at the foot of the cliff.

Birling Gap

We descend to the Gap (a lonely cluster of low, weather-worn buildings around a car park) across a small patch of unusual terrain: chalk heath. In the spring and summer months you'll tramp from Beachy Head among herbs and vetches, harebells and round-headed rampions, but at this point you come across clumps of gorse and heather. The chalk here is covered with a layer of sandy loess, blown in from the dry floor of the North Sea during the last glacial period. The odd result is that acid-lovers such as heathers and tormentil grow side by side with the likes of thyme, salad burnet and dropwort, which have adapted to the chalk.

The single-storey, timber-planked Birling Gap Hotel, which describes itself as a Victorian colonial-style villa, looks like the relic of a wild west frontier town – the frontier in this case being the greedy sea. A notice by the steps which lead down to the shingle reads: 'Please do not remove stones or pebbles from the beach', but if this is intended to preserve the cliff's precarious defences it's a desperate whistling in the dark. Photographs on display in the hotel reveal that houses along here have fallen into the sea well within living memory, and the National Trust, which owns most of the hamlet, has given up on the row of houses (six left at present, including the coastguard's headquarters) which face the elements end-on. One of them is called Mermaids, and all will before very long find themselves communing with the seashells and seaweed at the bottom of the ocean.

The Trust and English Nature (now Natural England) fought local plans to build a protective rock wall, arguing that it would detract from the biological and geological interest of the area and that the cliffs at Birling Gap 'provide the best example of a cross-section through a dry valley anywhere in Britain'. Whatever you think about the geology v. wallbuilding question, this is certainly the best beach in the area for exploring rocks and hunting for fossils, with the ridges and gullies of a wave-cut platform extending some way out from the cliffs. Fossil aficionados say that the best places to look are around the great boulders on the beach: if you're lucky you'll find some fine ribbed echinoids, also known as sea urchins, or shepherd's crowns.

Cuckmere Haven

An arduous switchback hike over the Seven Sisters is rewarded by a first glimpse of the one undeveloped rivermouth on the Sussex coast. The meanders of the Cuckmere River (*never* the River Cuckmere, please note) were bypassed by a swift-flowing cut in the 1840s, and the overused word 'iconic' can fairly be used of the view of their still blue waters against brilliant white cliffs which appears in so many books and calendars. Snake river, indeed!

But there's an ideological battle for the future of the coast here, too, with more dramatic implications than at Birling Gap. Since global warming is likely to raise sea and river levels later this century, the Environment Agency plans to walk away from costly flood protection work. At present the river flows to the sea between earth banks, timber walls and beach groynes: if these defences were breached, a tidal estuary would be created, as in former times, with areas of intertidal saltmarsh and mudflats.

The river valley would have a different kind of beauty, floral and faunal, and perhaps the meanders would flow again, at least until the waters rose to fill the natural basin between the hills. But public outrage is understandable, whatever the rights and wrongs of it. On fine weekends there's a cavalcade of walkers and cyclists along the paths by the river to the shingle beach beneath the cliffs – and the place still retains a blessed tranquillity. Better still, on a weekday I've found myself completely alone on the foreshore, with no sound but the waves and the gulls.

By the A259 there's a Seven Sisters Country Park visitor centre, with displays about local geology and wildlife. You can stop here for a cup of tea, take a walk around the park, canoe around the Cuckmere meanders, or hire a bicycle from the neighbouring Cuckmere Cycle Hire Shop. On the downland, a little to the south-east of the visitor centre are the footings of Exceat Church, the sole remains of a village probably wiped out by French raiders in the 14th century, while behind it rises the largely deciduous Friston Forest with the pretty flint village of West Dean comfortably tucked inside. It's a magical area.

Seaford Head

Climb the hill to the west of the Cuckmere and you pass a row of coastguard cottages on your way to the top of the Seaford Head nature reserve: the view back to the rivermouth is another familiar chocolate-box shot, used in the 2007 film *Atonement* as a symbol of nostalgic Englishness. You can now take the steep steps down to the fossil-rich beach at Hope Gap or press on via the Vanguard Way (more prehistoric humps and bumps here) towards the breezy golf course. Here there are large areas of the sandy deposits we noticed at Birling Gap, and the acid eats into the cliffs below to create so-called solution pipes in the chalk.

Make the most of the serenity: from this point the Sussex coast is built up for miles and miles and miles.

❯ The South Downs Way continues to Alfriston. The High Street is close-packed with old houses, while a large green (the Tye) fronts two 14th-century buildings – the large church and the thatched Clergy House, a Wealden hall house which was the first property bought by the fledgling National Trust back in 1896.

A TALE OF TWO HARBOURS

SEAFORD TO NEWHAVEN

The power of the sea is a recurring theme of our journey. To descend the gentle green slope from Seaford Head to the exposed seafront below is to be confronted with further evidence of its ability to transform not only the landscape but the course of human lives.

Seaford

At the eastern end of the beach is Splash Point, and it was here that the River Ouse ran down to the sea from Lewes during medieval times. Seaford then was a prosperous port, providing five ships and 80 men for the Cinque Ports fleet in 1347, but today there's not a trace of harbour or trade.

The usual culprits were responsible for its demise: French raiders, the Black Death and, especially, the silting up of the harbour. The river originally approached from the north-west some 3 miles (5 km) away at Denton, but later it took a more direct route to the sea near the village of Meeching, and during the 17th century a 'new haven' was developed there – you can see its modern harbour arms under the cliffs to the west. The locals took to smuggling and wrecking instead.

The Esplanade

We have to thank this ancient abandonment for today's seafront – which is plain, but unspoilt – because the town never really recovered. There was a flurry of relative prosperity after the railway came in 1864: like

Bexhill, Seaford attracted a host of boarding schools, all but one of which have closed, and Edward VII stayed at the Esplanade Hotel (gone, too) in 1905. Then more Edwardian slumber.

At Splash Point a colourful signboard illustrates some of the things we might look out for on the shingle, such as the eggs cases of whelks (those familiar yellow honeycombs) and dogfish (the so-called mermaids' purses). Plants to look out for between here and Newhaven include sea kale, yellow horned poppy, biting stonecrop, sea campion and orache, and it's the habitat of (harmless) jumping spiders, too.

Another sign promotes a circular 5-mile (8-km) 'exercise path', via Tide Mills to the west – and it does indeed feel healthy to inhale lungfuls of the salt air flying in across Seaford Bay, with cliffs to east and west and no commercial clutter to divert you on the way.

Landwards, too, there's space. New terraces of flats have sprouted in recent years, but – and especially at the eastern end – undeveloped fields fall away from the road, with the town beginning a spacious distance away. Presumably this shocking lack of development can't last, so enjoy Seaford's rawness while you can.

Seaford museum
Martello tower number 74 has a cannon on top and houses a museum with a difference. It records the town's story from Cinque Port days and displays the relics of some of the many shipwrecks off the coast, but it's busy with living history, too: wartime memorabilia, early computers rescued from local offices, projectors from the old Ritz cinema, recreated shops, a working model of the railway station in 1926 and so on. It's closed more often than it's open, but drop in if you can – and say farewell to the Martello chain, since this is the most westerly of them, and therefore the last we shall see.

Tide Mills
And so we proceed (jogging or otherwise) to an industrial relic of the 18th and 19th centuries. The scourings of the sea created a large tidal creek behind the shingle bank east of Newhaven, and a tide mill was

built here in 1761. It had five pairs of millstones, and you can still see three wheel tunnels in the dam and the remnants of the sluice gate.

Tidal energy allowed the mills to be used for all of 16 hours a day, and the village was about a 100 strong in its heyday, with barges taking grain upriver to Lewes and larger ships carrying it away by sea. In 1795 it played its part in a mutiny, when members of the Oxford militia, housed locally in appalling conditions, commandeered a sloop and filled it with about 300 sacks of flour: after the uprising was over, two men were executed at Brighton.

Although Tide Mills later had its own railway halt on the line between Newhaven and Seaford (a large concrete signboard stands close to the crossing gates, the name faded), it was the new age of steam which killed the business, since farmers found it cheaper to transport their grain by goods wagons, to be milled further afield.

The mills had closed by 1890, but a small community continued to live here in spartan conditions (there was no running water) until World War II, when the army blasted the buildings away so that invading forces couldn't use them. Today you can walk the empty streets among the sorry stumps of the buildings.

Chailey Heritage, the charity which Grace Kimmins founded in central Sussex to educate children with a range of physical ailments, opened a marine hospital on the shingle during the 1920s, and its footings can be seen a little to the south-east of the mill ruins.

Newhaven

Newhaven is a ferry port, and that's its embarrassment. Four hours across the water lies Dieppe, a town for which the phrase Gallic charm might have been invented – pretty little cobbled streets lined with patisseries and boutiques running down to a quayside of aromatic restaurants and small shops.

And Newhaven? Its high street, a long way inland, was long ago cut short and surrounded by a veritable race-track for cars on their way to anywhere but here. Inside this snarling whirlpool you find ugly, unloved buildings, several of them closed and wall-eyed, their windows whitewashed over. Perhaps these are earmarked for demolition and replacement, because the town is the subject of a 'regeneration project' which involves 'initiatives', ghastly acronym clusters and some money. It's not before time, because the people look defeated, the economy shot.

Meanwhile, in case the locals get too excited about this, the County Council has compulsorily purchased land at North Quay, above the swing bridge, so that it can build a large waste incinerator which protesters claim will impair the health of thousands for many miles around.

There's a thrilling dynamism about a bustling commercial port, but this one has undeniably gone to seed. We hope to lift our spirits by heading towards the sea along West Quay, with the ferry terminal on the far bank, but then we get a pretty good idea of what regeneration means. This is where the local fishermen moor their boats, and there's a strange disjunction between these leather-skinned seamen among their ropes and lobster pots and the sudden gentrification of the area on to which they step ashore.

Close by there are tasteful slate signs, with English on one side and French on the other, pointing out the historical significance of the area. The fishermen have been given a new market hall, there's a new lifeboat station and, close to the well-stocked yacht marina, tall, balconied blocks of flats are going up 'in a style to evoke fishing lofts'. There are viewing areas, soon there will be a few shops and only the well-heeled will be able to live here.

Sovereign Harbour at Eastbourne is artificial swankiness created where there was nothing save bare shingle before. Newhaven will have a small equivalent on a harbourside which will have lost its authenticity.

◉ Up on the cliff, on a spot defended since the Bronze Age, sits the largest fortification ever built in Sussex. Newhaven Fort, fully restored and open during the season, dates from the 1860s. You can explore gun emplacements, bunkers and some of the vast, echoing tunnels that run through the hillside to the western foreshore.

LAND OF THE FREE

UP-RIVER TO LEWES

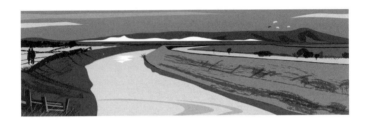

Work-a-day, sleeves-rolled, clocking-on Lewes may be largely a memory, but to approach it along the riverbank from the south is to be reminded that the Ouse was for centuries an industrial thoroughfare and that the capital of East Sussex (of *all* Sussex, locals would claim) earned its living from it until well into the 20th century.

The nature reserve on your left, with kingfishers flashing over the brooks, is on the site of former railway sidings and a freight depot which served the Southerham quarries to the east. There was a boat repair yard at the little cutting now used by Lewes Rowing Club, and some of the house names in South Street (the main road to Eastbourne until the Cuilfail tunnel was burrowed through the chalk in 1980) are reminders of those bustling times: Bargemaster's House, Boat House, Paymaster's Cottage, The Old Union Master's. Local pubs included the Bargeman's Arms, the Ship and the Schooner.

This is the Cliffe area of the town, historically separate (until 1881) and proud of it: the Norman rape of Pevensey had the river as its western boundary. From the pretty 18th-century bridge you can see, on both banks of the river, more evidence of trade and commerce in the port of Lewes – although warehouses have been turned into luxury homes and several former riparian businesses, including the Phoenix Ironworks, are long gone.

Still with us, though, is Harvey's, the last remaining brewery in Sussex, whose chimney suffuses the air with deep flavours of malt and hops several times a week.

One-offs

The county town straddles a spur of the Downs, is close-packed with ancient higgledy-piggledy houses, has narrow twittens winding south from the spine of its high street between high flint walls and, accommodating a population of about 16,000, is agreeably intimate in size.

It also retains some individuality. Before you cross the bridge, put your nose into Bill's Produce Store where, among more prosaic varieties, you might seek out ten types of cucumber, 20 kinds of tomato, strange-looking wild mushrooms you've never set eyes on before and black truffles priced to make your bank manager wince. There are quiches made on the premises, a range of continental breads and colourful jars of preserves piled to the ceiling.

Bill's, in short, epitomises the independent shopping experience of Lewes, in which antique shops, second-hand book sellers, delicatessens and restaurants have flourished in recent years. Few of the chains are represented here, and some of the shop window displays are so enigmatic that you're hard-pressed to guess what they sell (in most cases, everything from the pressed flowers and the back-scratchers to the books and the carving knives).

The awkward squad

This may be a gentle place, but the locals take something of a pride in their reputation for stroppiness. Within three years of parking meters being introduced in the autumn of 2004 almost a hundred of them were blown up beyond repair, another 170 were crippled and a reward of £5,000 was posted in an attempt to nail the culprits. While respectable citizens lamented the cost of this criminal damage (some £300,000), not to speak of the danger involved, one sensed a suppressed glee beneath their routine expressions of disapproval. Hilariously, the managers of the parking scheme switched the traffic wardens' comic opera uniforms from bright red to blue in the belief that this would calm the anger of bullish motorists. They don't look you in the eye.

Lewes is well-stocked with explosives, as its six bonfire societies mount the country's most spectacular bonfire celebrations every November, and any event of note in the town is marked with a firework display. The 'bonfire boys' remember not only the scuppering of Guy Fawkes's plot but the courage of the martyrs burned to death outside what is now the town hall in the reign of the Catholic Mary. Lewes was defiantly protestant then, just as it was staunchly on the Parliament side against the King in the Civil War and was recognised to be a hotbed of puritanism and non-conformism.

And then there was the great radical writer and promoter of revolutions Thomas Paine, who debated politics during meetings of the Headstrong Club at the White Hart hotel, who lived near the castle at Bull House with a wife he later deserted, and who wrote his first pamphlet while he was here – albeit one in support of a pay rise for customs officers, of whom he was one, rather than for the grand cause of liberty. Tom Paine is an unofficially adopted son of Lewes, who silently gives his blessing every time grim authority is given a stick in the eye.

The castle

Simon de Montfort was another rebel who made an impact on the town, taking the castle from Henry III in 1264 and forcing on him various concessions (through the Mise of Lewes) which are regarded as early milestones on the long and winding road to democracy. Built for the Conqueror, it has a 14th century barbican and, unusually, two 'mottes' or mounds – one a little way off and now outside its grounds, and the other surmounted by the impressive keep. The views from here are superb: William Morris wrote of Lewes 'lying like a box of toys under a great amphitheatre of chalk hills'.

◗ Bartholomew House, by the castle entrance, is one of many buildings in the centre of Lewes faced with mathematical tiles – or 'M tiles' to the cognoscenti. In the Georgian era, when bricks were all the rage, existing buildings would often have these brick look-alikes affixed to their fronts. Bartholomew House has black tiles, but most were terracotta to look like the real thing.

LURELAND

PEACEHAVEN TO ROTTINGDEAN

Before World War I there was scarcely a building on the turfy clifftops between Newhaven and Rottingdean. Then along came the brash developer Charles Neville, and a bungaloid rash spread like a contagion until it filled every rise and hollow. For those who live here it is no doubt a little heaven (the Downs behind, the sea below), but it's every planner's nightmare.

Peacehaven

Peacehaven, running into Telscombe Cliffs, is the very worst of it. Stand by the Greenwich meridian marker near the cliff edge and you're on Neville's promenade – nothing but a rough track. He did build a sumptuous hotel, now demolished, but his new settlement was a do-it-yourself kind of place, especially in the early years, and it never lived up to his mouth-watering hype.

The first settlers arrived in 1921, to find little but a grid of dirt roads with empty housing plots on which they could erect pretty much what they wanted. (The actress Dame Flora Robson, who lived here briefly as a teenager, later recalled her father's disgust when a neighbour camped out in a bicycle shed.) Neville was selling the dream of 'a garden city by the sea', which he also called Lureland, and he took out advertisements and ran competitions in the national press. The reality was a rudimentary water supply, intermittent electric lighting and cess-pit sanitation.

Since Peacehaven lay between the jurisdictions of Newhaven and Brighton there was at first no police force, so Neville created his own, putting a couple of men in uniform and giving them a Model T Ford to run around in. Other staff made do with horses, and early pictures posed outside the clapboard company offices look like scenes from the Wild West. There was no doctor, no school, and people living on the remoter edges of the development would run up a flag to attract visiting tradesmen. Many of the plots lay vacant for many years, and neighbours fenced them off until they became the owners by virtue of squatters' rights.

Saltdean

The lie of the land dictated a sinuous street plan for Saltdean, rather than a grid as at Peacehaven. During the 1930s it was given a modernist touch, with 'Hollywood modern' bungalows (white walls and green roofs) and others in Italian, Spanish and cubist styles.

Two typical 1930s buildings have triumphantly survived periods of neglect: the Grand Ocean Hotel (now apartments), with its confident curved front and roof-garden sundecks, and Saltdean Lido on the main coast road – more curves, glass, steel and sweeping terraces.

Rottingdean

Neville also built at Rottingdean (his Tudor Close Hotel, long gone, attracted film stars such as Bette Davis and Cary Grant), but it would be unfair to tar the village with the Lureland brush. It had grown organically from Saxon times, and the books of Bob Copper, who grew up here in the 1930s, reveal how isolated it was, even in living memory, with farms up on the slopes and a fishing community down at the coast.

There's a pretty area around the Green, with the flint church looking down on a pond flanked by fine old houses. Rudyard Kipling lived briefly at The Elms, and his uncle, the artist Edward Burne-Jones, owned North End House close by.

❯ Set into the wall outside The Elms is 'the wishing stone'. It looks for all the world like a little face and supposedly has magical properties. This is, of course, a nonsense – although when I once took a photograph of it the film instantly rewound in my camera.

L O N D O N - B Y - T H E - S E A

B R I G H T O N & H O V E

The coast road to Brighton takes you below the black smock mill on the golf course at Rottingdean, the large 'international modern' St Dunstan's building of 1938 at Ovingdean and the imposing bulk of the famous girls' boarding school at Roedean. Our preferred route, however, is to descend to the beach by the White Horse Inn at Rottingdean and pick up the undercliff walk which begins east at Saltdean and will now take us west to Brighton Marina.

The rows of concrete blocks you see at low tide off Rottingdean are the remnants of the ambitious and short-lived 'Daddy Longlegs' railway devised by the inventor and electrical pioneer Magnus Volk. It opened in 1896, carrying passengers between Brighton and Rottingdean on the Pioneer, a ship-like deck on stilts high above the waves, but the building of sea defences a little to the west in 1901 forced its closure.

We're walking on a sea wall created in the 1930s. There are rock pools on the beach below, with gullies and ridges created over millennia in a wave-cut platform. The chalk cliffs on our right-hand side – buttressed and netted to prevent dangerous falls – are the last we shall see on our journey, and they change in colour and form as we draw level with the marina.

Here, some 15 ft (4.5 m) above our heads on a chalk base, is a 'raised beach' originally laid down some 100,000 years ago during a warm lull in the last ice age. Its sandy gravels contain worn and rounded flint

[67]

pebbles, and the jawbone of a whale has been found in it. Above it is a thicker layer of glacial deposits – a chalky rubble known as coombe rock – which has yielded the remains of primitive horses, mammoths and woolly rhinos. This short section of cliff, a mere 200 yds (183 m) in extent, is a protected geological feature.

Brighton Marina

A marina without a view of the sea is a strange notion, and one without a sight of boats is weirder still. That's the experience of motorists passing through the ghastly concrete tunnels and down the concrete ramp to the (free) concrete car park with its neighbouring fast-food restaurants, Bowplex, Cineworld and Asda supermarket. It's a vision of hell, and a frank admission that 'the south coast's ultimate waterfront destination', as the pamphlets ludicrously have it, is in reality a cynical retail and property development exercise.

The advantage of walking past it below the cliffs is that you do see something just a little better. Low-rise, yellow-bricked, faux-Georgian shops, flats and houses are grouped around small squares; motor launches cluster in pockets of the inner harbour; a 'boardwalk', lined with restaurants, looks down on the outer harbour chockful of yachts, their riggings tinkling in the breeze; there's the rump of a once proud fishing fleet; and you can hire a boat for sightseeing, to go diving or to catch mackerel.

It could have been so much better, but the truth is that since being opened by the Queen in 1979 this intended 'city by the sea' has not only been developed in fits and starts but is already officially in need of regeneration. Since Brighton is currently going through a 'build 'em high' phase, it's not surprising that a 42-storey tower block is in the offing – although the then environment secretary originally stipulated that buildings shouldn't rise more than half the height of the cliff behind. Money talks, and these days talks big.

Along Madeira Drive

West out of the marina we reach Black Rock, and the terminus of Magnus Volk's other, more successful transport system. Volk's Railway, the first public electric railway in the country, was launched in 1883, and its open-sided carriages with their brown and yellow livery still run during the season to an attractive little station just west of the pier.

The Black Rock area itself is a sorry dead end (its popular swimming pool closed back in 1978), although the skaters Jayne Torvill and Robin Cousins are behind plans for an events arena here which would include two Olympic ice pads – oh, and 109 residential apartments, '40 per cent of which will be affordable housing'.

As we walk alongside the endless shingle, an area of which was declared an official nudist beach on April Fool's day 1980, we might well wish ourselves up above with the motorists on Marine Parade. They'll be entering Brighton past the beautiful Georgian squares and terraces of Kemp Town, most of them developed for Thomas Read Kemp by the architects Charles Busby, Amon Wilds and his son Amon Henry Wilds.

But never mind: their high road sweeps down to the aquarium and the pier, and we shall meet it there via the splendid filigree arches of Madeira Drive. These support the 'first floor' Madeira Terrace, more than half a mile (0.8 km) long, built against the great sea wall in 1890. The ornate, canopied and now disused Madeira Lift was installed at the same time, to take passengers up to Marine Parade.

If Madeira Drive looks like a race track, so it has often been, with speed trials over measured distances. It's also the destination of many events between London and Brighton, including annual runs for veteran cars, commercial vehicles and bicycles. Having completed the London-Brighton cycle ride a few times myself, I can assure you that it's an exhilarating feeling to sweep along the 'home straight' to the finishing line after a few hours in the saddle.

Around the pier

And so to the beating heart of the place. Yes, we're at the eastern end of town, but this busy area – four roads converging; the Royal Albion Hotel at the seaward end of the Old Steine; the Sea Life Centre in the Victorian aquarium to one side, its vaulted underground ceiling supported by marble and granite columns; the pier thronged with visitors – sets the tone for footloose, anything-goes, hedonistic Brighton.

The Palace Pier is everything a pier should be. (Forgive me for using the original name, but its recent reincarnation as Brighton Pier sticks in the craw, smacking as it does of the owners' triumphalism over the demise of the West Pier, its last, rusted girders still visible as I write – but soon no more.) It's a seaside fantasy, with an oriental theme, an elaborate clock tower, filigree arches, flags, domes, kiosks, and – at the far end of its 1,650-ft (500-m) length – a complete funfair, with dodgems, a ghost train, a big dipper and the latest in daredevil, disorientating, hurl-yourself-into-the-skies rides. There are, of course, arcade amusements, restaurants and bars a-plenty, and if you can't get some pleasure from an hour or two on the teak decking you shouldn't be in Brighton at all.

Ah, Brighton! *The Argus* regularly prints letters from readers lamenting a sorry decline in standards of street cleanliness, transport or whatever, but this is to fall into the error of thinking that this is their town just because they pay the rates. Everybody else knows that it belongs to the world, and that the world dances in and out of its pleasures without a thought to those who live here. There may be something laughably self-important about its recently acquired city status (as if it needed some external blessing, after all), but it is, indeed, London-by-the-Sea.

Outsiders transformed it in the first place, finding it just right for redevelopment. Eighteenth-century Brighton was not the fishing village of romantic legend but a once prosperous town (the largest in Sussex), brought low by the washing away of its foreshore and the decline of its fishing fleet. Then 'fashion' flocked to it, some for the sea-water cure and others simply to be seen, and the population soared from some 6,000 in 1794 to more than 24,000 by 1821, and (after the arrival of the railway) to 65,000 by 1851.

Graham Greene famously brought to life its 1930s' seediness in *Brighton Rock* – and fittingly set its culminating murder in potholed Peacehaven. The place has changed a great deal since those days of razor gangs and one-night sexual encounters for the benefit of divorce lawyers, but it retains a definite edge. Actors, artists, journalists and other vagabonds fall in love with it. You slip the usual rules when you come here: no wonder that it was an early refuge for the once oppressed gay community, which in today's unfettered times celebrates itself with a flamboyant Gay Pride carnival every year.

From the pier you can walk west along King's Road (the Grand and the Metropole are the most imposing of the hotels), or descend to the lower esplanade. The council has been spending money here in recent years, and a paved path passes seafront arches which are a home to bars and restaurants, a fishing museum and an artists' quarter.

Decimus Burton's West Pier, then the only Grade I listed pier in the country, closed in 1975. It was a real beauty, and it's still almost beyond belief that it was allowed to decay and, finally, to succumb to fire as well as rust: it's now nothing but a cage squatting in the water. There are currently plans to erect a kind of London Eye at the landward end (same architects, but this time a doughnut-shaped observation platform). The local protests are understandable because of its great height, but offbeat Brighton will no doubt happily accommodate it.

The Royal Pavilion

The Prince Regent's oriental hallucination, a few hundred yards up the Steine from the aquarium, is the ultimate in seaside architecture and is surely so extreme as to be above criticism. Of course people have laughed at its Indian exoticism without and Chinese dazzle within, but the future George IV was sufficiently educated in the arts to know that he was enjoying himself at the expense of refined taste. He apparently cried for joy when his palace was finished.

At the centre of the banqueting room's great domed ceiling is a branching plantain tree, under which a winged and silvered dragon with fiery tongue grasps the top of a vast 30-ft (9-m) chandelier in its claws. The music room – crimson and gold landscape murals, huge serpents and dragons – has a dome of gilded scallop-shaped scales above a coving painted in brilliant patterns of blue and gold. (Rossini entertained the company here over Christmas 1823.) More humble, but still magnificent in its own way, is the great kitchen, in which a dozen cooks at a time would work – the original range and spit are still in place.

Into Hove

We leave Brighton itself at the Peace memorial. The refurbished Embassy Court lies on the other side of King's Road (a striking 11-storey, 1930s block of flats, with wide concrete balconies), and soon, beginning with Brunswick Terrace, we arrive at some outstanding Regency squares and terraces – Wilds and Busby again.

These are magnificent, but poor old Hove can't help but seem a dull stick compared with its once neighbour and now corporate spouse. Even the landscape has changed, the chalk having receded and never to be seen at close quarters again. From this point in our journey we're on the so-called coastal plain, a wedge of flat and fertile land which geologically falls outside the Wealden anticline of sand, clay and chalk. It's proved irresistible to builders.

After Brighton's chatter, the seafront at Hove is a gentle murmur – lawns, children's play areas and the shallow waters of the lagoon. But wait for it: the worn-out King Alfred Leisure Centre, at the western end, is about to be replaced by a 'courageous' complex of sports facilities and housing (all crinkled towers and coloured panels) designed by Frank Gehry – he of the great eye-catchers in Bilbao, Seattle and Las Vegas.

In Hove, actually?

❧

❯ Visit Palmeira Square, in Hove, in drought conditions and you may make out a circular pattern in the turf. This is the outline of the Anthaeum, the largest glass dome in the world when it was erected here in 1833 to house a tropical garden. Alas, it collapsed two days before its official opening, and the wreckage lay in the square for more than 20 years.

UP-AND-COMING

SHOREHAM

The word is out that Shoreham is the new 'place to be', although those of us who have long known its secrets wonder what will become of its louche charm once the developers get to work.

To approach from the east is to wonder what all the fuss is about. You can walk the waterfront from Hove seawards of the harbour, but your 2-mile (3.2-km) hike to the east breakwater (via the fringes of Portslade and into West Sussex at Southwick) is overshadowed by a power station chimney and the bleak buildings and heaps of waste you'd expect of an industrial site. The journey by road is little better, although you do get occasional glimpses of dredgers and cargo boats.

Centuries ago shingle drift turned the River Adur eastward just short of the coast, and Shoreham Harbour now stretches for some 4 miles (6.4 km), with its opening a little to the west of centre (a trim little 1840s lighthouse stands opposite, close to the A259) and its chief working area to the east. It's not as busy as it was even within living memory, although it still shifts 15 per cent of the nation's grain exports, but a transformation awaits. Here, we're told by the South East England Development Agency (SEEDA), up to 10,000 new homes are to be planted, creating 7,750 new jobs, along with – count the clichés – 'sustainable transport links, community, education and health facilities, leading to the creation of a thriving, state-of-the-art sustainable community on the Sussex coast'.

The old town

Swing round the corner past the Sussex Yacht Club and you're driving into the short High Street of Shoreham itself. North of it lies an informal grid of lanes, lined with terraces of humble cottages – a good deal of flint – and overlooked by the great 12th-century tower of St Mary de Haura ('of the harbour') Church. The nave was destroyed long ago, but this was a massive building and the congregation now worships in the arcaded splendour of what was originally the choir.

Venerable though it is, this is the church of New Shoreham. To the north-east, overlooking the tidal reaches of the river, with Lancing College chapel high on the Downs beyond, is Old Shoreham church, St Nicholas – an engaging cruciform building with some finely carved Norman arches inside. (The nave arch has a cat's face on top.) The restored 500-ft (152-m) wooden bridge close by was the only one across the lower Adur until the first Norfolk Bridge was built downstream in 1833, and it carried traffic until as recently as 1970.

The original town lay here – St Nicholas is Saxon in origin – but as early as 1100 the silting of the estuary prompted the Normans to transfer their harbour activities to New Shoreham instead.

High Street

You could call the centre of Shoreham dowdy, but it's simply a place that has been allowed to potter on its riverside way without any fuss. Slipways run down from the High Street to the sluggish Adur, where fishing boats bob at anchor and canoeists paddle leisurely by. The Crown and Anchor pub may now be 'gastro', but it still sports its luridly painted ship's figurehead outside.

The chequer-faced Marlipins is one of the oldest secular buildings in Sussex. It's owned by the Sussex Archaeological Society, which added a two-storey annexe in 2004 and has created a range of local history displays. The Marlipins is Norman (although its facade dates from the 14th century) and may have been a customs house for the new port. Across the road you'll find a late Georgian customs house which was converted into the town hall in 1886 and is now an Italian restaurant.

At the western end of the street, by the Norfolk Bridge, is Ropetackle, for many years a fishermen's hard, but now a SEEDA-blessed development reminiscent of the marinas at Eastbourne and Brighton, albeit without the docked boats. There's a lot of yellow brick, narrow eaves, weatherboarding and flint panels; there are riverside walks, shops, cafés and 'public open spaces'; there's an arts, education and business centre – and the locals don't much like it.

Shoreham Beach

A footbridge from the High Street takes you across to Shoreham Beach. It's not quite an island, but it has a little of that cut-off, free-from-all-shackles feeling. Houseboats are moored along one bank, some with small gardens – and one using old enamel urinals as characterful plant pots.

Before wartime clearance this was a shanty town, and despite a few recent developments (what *is* it about yellow brick?) there's still an individuality in the varied styles of the bungalows: white-painted verandahs, solar panels, a Spanish hacienda here, an ultra-modern glass cabin there. Along Fort Road there's even a survivor of that rough-and-ready past: a liveried London, Brighton & South Coast Railway carriage still used as a home.

On the shingle by the harbour's west breakwater are the remains of Shoreham Redoubt, which was built in 1857 but never fired any of its six guns in anger. Its best known use was as an open-air studio for the wonderfully named Sunny South Film Company during World War I. The area was popular with early film-makers because of the good light, and actors, directors and their friends moved to 'bungalow town' on Shoreham Beach in large numbers.

Today this is a good spot for those who enjoy coastal desolation – a cold, grey sea, long stretches of bare shingle, the harbour and its light-house behind, birds passing overhead. The clangorous world is far away.

❯ Travelling west from Shoreham you'll be aware of a constant procession of light aircraft in the skies above you, on business, pleasure and training flights. You can enjoy the pretty little planes close at hand from the restaurant in Shoreham Airport's 1930s art deco terminal building – featured in countless period films.

A QUIET LIFE

AROUND WORTHING

D r Johnson, in one of his fine distinctions, spoke of a place being 'worth seeing, yes, but not worth *going* to see'. Alas, not only is there nothing worth going to see in the 10 miles (16 km) of bungaloid sprawl between Lancing and Rustington, but little worth seeing either – to which unkind remark many of its inhabitants would doubtless retort that they're blissfully content with their sedate seaside idyll and that it's no damn business of ours in any case.

Widewater Lagoon

And yet it begins well enough at Lancing. Sand which we find only at low tides further east is more in evidence here (and will become a major coastal feature as we journey west). Behind the beach huts, we find a landlocked stretch of brackish water with a row of luxurious houses clustered on its northern bank. Widewater Lagoon is a local nature reserve, its waters replenished by the sea at high tides, and visited by the likes of redshank, cormorants, grebe, little egrets, ducks and swans.

Worthing

It's easy to imagine Henry James strolling around Church Square at Rye and Graham Greene sipping a couple of gins in a Brighton bar, but Oscar Wilde and his green carnation at Worthing? (He wrote *The Importance of Being Earnest* here, and his leading character, famously discovered in a handbag at Victoria Station, is named after the town.) No, I'm afraid that it's an absurdity.

In the summer of 1798, George III's youngest daughter, Princess Amelia, visited Worthing to get over a forbidden affair with one of her father's equerries – and so, the story goes, brought the place a glamour which helped launch it as a resort. You may wonder what happened next, for Worthing doesn't really feel like a resort at all: it's a town which happens to sit by the sea.

Away from the seafront you may search out the Georgian grandeur of Liverpool Terrace and Park Crescent, and in recent years the council has pedestrianised large areas and furnished them with trees and comfortable benches. On the front itself, almost opposite the (drab) pier, is my nomination for the ugliest building anywhere on the Sussex coast – the grim bunker that is Knightsbridge House, with a supermarket below, a hideous multi-storey car park alongside and ten-pin bowling in the concrete ugliness behind. It's the worst of a bad bunch, sad to say. Worthing's planners have allowed a grievous amount of dross to sprout between earlier attempts at seaside elegance.

Seaweed

Between Shoreham and Littlehampton the sea is only 33 ft (10 m) deep 2 miles (3.2 km) offshore, and the sun-warmed seaweed thickens into blankets. After south-westerly gales it comes ashore at Worthing. It stinks, and it's alive with little flies which, although they don't sting or bite, dance around your face and get into your sandwiches.

The authorities have used flame-throwers and suction-dredgers, they've had farmers bag it up and take it away; they've tried pumping it and even blowing it up; but they can't crack the problem. No wonder the locals have taken shelter inland.

❥ There are two curiosities to look out for at Goring, west of Worthing. What's billed as 'the longest ilex avenue in the world' (comprising more than 450 evergreens) runs from Sea Lane in Goring to Sea Lane in Ferring. And at the English Martyrs Roman Catholic Church you can crane your neck to a bravura replica of Michelangelo's Sistine Chapel ceiling, courtesy of the signwriter Gary Bevans. It took him more than five years to complete.

TO THE ARUN & BEYOND
LITTLEHAMPTON TO BOGNOR

The Downs are still a presence behind Worthing, but they soon become far distant and we're walking flatlands once covered by the sea and vulnerable to it still. Although you can't, of course, hear the legendary muffled sounds of drowned church bells, there are lost village streets under the waves out there, and roads which now stop at the sea once continued on their way south for a mile or more.

Littlehampton

And what sand! At Littlehampton it stretches away so far to a rippling low tide that you walk for minutes across the wormcasts for a dip – and then it takes an age to kick your way through the shallows until the water's deep enough to swim in.

The front here is 1¹/₂ miles (2.4 km) east to west, and in high season the beach is such a swarm of sun-loving flesh that the council offers a free 'child tag' scheme so that a tearful foundling can be returned to the colour-coded part of the beach it came from. (Parents can put their mobile number on it for swift results.)

Behind the beach is The Green, a broad area which in Eastbourne would be landscaped and planted, but which here is what the name implies – an expanse innocent of anything but grass. It gives the front a wonderfully airy feel. There were sand dunes here until late in the 19th century when the 15th Duke of Norfolk had the ground flattened and seeded in order to create work for the unemployed. Further behind are the first houses. In 1790 the Earl of Berkeley launched Littlehampton as a fashionable watering place, although it never aspired to the dangerous delights of a Brighton. A relative prosperity in Georgian times can be seen in the attractive balconied houses of South Terrace, which were developed from east to west over several decades.

The East Beach Café

Into this unpretentious holidayscape has been planted a striking elongated, low-level building which has had architects drooling. The East Beach Café (designer Thomas Heatherwick) is made of bronze-washed patinated steel, its land-facing side a series of armadillo-like plates, its seaward front almost uninterrupted glass. One critic suggested that by inspiration alone it might galvanise 'narcoleptic' Littlehampton, although it's perhaps a bit much to expect so much of one small building on such a lengthy promenade.

But wait: the food is rather above the bucket-and-spade norm, too. After all, the café's inaugural chef, David Whiteside, has 'cooking at the Ritz' on his CV. The place was close to full, although it was out of season, when I first went in to order that true test of seaside cuisine, fish and chips. The price was (of course) at least twice what you'd pay at a cheap and cheerful restaurant in town, and the chips were presented in an aluminium mess-tin (you know the kind of thing), but the fish was beautifully prepared and was washed down by a very acceptable cup of tea. I'll go again.

By the river

The Arun, the swiftest of our Sussex rivers, meets the sea at the west of the town – nothing has been developed beyond it. The main port was up-river at Arundel, but Littlehampton had a thriving shipbuilding industry in the 18th century and there were wharves on its eastern bank until a few years ago.

When I was a kid, our South London youth club would bring us down to Littlehampton for the day, with half-price tickets to go on the funfair rides. The roller coaster on its massive wooden trestles has disappeared, but the amusements are still in full swing, along with a theatre and a cinema.

Elsewhere, however, things have changed. There's now a designated riverside walk to the centre of town, tastefully paved and with, at intervals, slate roundels sprouting shells like wings and inscribed with seafood recipes. The old warehouses have been replaced by the kind of harbour-style seafront buildings we've become familiar with on our journey (although, on a bend in the river, they look more authentic here than anywhere else), and there's a 'Look and Sea!' (sorry) shop-cum-museum with a viewing gallery above.

Littlehampton Fort

Across the river, within the golf course, are the overgrown remains of a fort built in 1854, and so a cousin of the one we found at Shoreham Beach. (An earlier battery had been built on the east bank in the 1750s, the mound still visible among the amusements.) It was armed with five guns, each capable of firing up to 1,600 yds (1,460 m), and its two underground magazines could house 126 barrels of gunpowder, but it was abandoned within 20 years.

Bailiffscourt

On Littlehampton's west beach we're at last away from coastal housing sprawl, and when – after a couple of miles – we do once more come across a collection of buildings, it's to shake our heads in bewilderment. The hamlet of Atherington is in Climping parish, and on its western fringes, just in from the coastline, is the strange throwback of Bailiffscourt – a range of 'medieval' buildings and a moat. It's now a hotel, so you're free to take a look.

The estate was originally owned by the bailiff of the abbey of Séez in Normandy, and the late 13th-century chapel in the grounds was here then. Everything else is the legacy of Lord Moyne and his architect Amyas Phillips from 1935 onwards. Some of the buildings were brought in from outside (as at the Weald and Downland open-air museum at

Singleton) but others were lovingly built from scratch in medieval style but incorporating some genuine window frames, carvings and so on from elsewhere. The main building is in the style of a 15th-century west country farmhouse, with a Horsham slab roof. There's a granary on staddlestones, a thatched cottage, a brick and half-timber gatehouse – and much more.

Rock Island Line

Back in 1753 an early map-maker noted that the church at Middleton-on-Sea was 'in danger of being washed away', while later in the century the poet Charlotte Smith (whose work was valued by Wordsworth) found only two or three houses still standing, the waves but a few feet from the half-ruined church and graves being carried out to sea:

> *The wild blast, rising from the western cave,*
> *Drives the huge billows from their heaving bed;*
> *Tears from their grassy tombs the village dead,*
> *And breaks the silent sabbath of the grave!*

That church, along with a good deal of coastal Middleton, is indeed long gone – its replacement dates from 1849 – but the locals are still battling against the elements. (The place had a revival in the 1920s, and there's now a population of around 5,000.) You'll see the latest, highly unusual defences as you walk along the beach towards Felpham, where William Blake lived for a time. Eight substantial rock islands were planted just offshore in the early 1990s, and the scalloped indentations of the sands behind them reveal how effective they've been.

Bognor Regis

And so, welcomed by the white canopies of the Butlins 'skyline pavil-ion', we reach the last of the resorts on our westerly journey. Billy Butlin himself designed the holiday camp which grew here from 1950 on the site of a former aircraft factory. It's probably the jolliest part of town.

Poor Bognor. George V sanctioned the 'Regis' suffix after recuperating from a serious illness at Craigweil House nearby, but whether or not he ever uttered that 'bugger Bognor' imprecation which the town will never live down, someone seems to have taken him at his word.

Most seaside resorts have a fairly long and straight promenade. You don't think about this until you come to Bognor, whose seafront snakes just enough to refuse any continuity. The pier, although Grade 2 listed, is in a bad way, its end fenced off. The Royal Hotel opposite has a fetching facade – pastel shades, a columned entrance, cast-iron balconies – but the area is generally dismal.

Will there be something better around the corner? Not really. There are signs of what might have been (perhaps was?) a predominant architectural motif in occasional houses with ornate verandahs, but these are shouldered out by too many unremarkable neighbours. The Steyne, with its bow-fronted and balconied terraces around a narrow green, is the best it gets. The low-slung Royal Norfolk Hotel is an attractive, if a little severe, stucco building with pediments and nine Italianate bays, but it's set well back from the front at an angle as if it doesn't really want to be a part of the scene.

Hothampton

The most interesting parts of Bognor lie off the front, being the remnants of the fashionable town which the London hatter Sir Richard Hotham began to create between 1785 and his death in 1799. He hoped that it would become known as Hothampton, but it rather fizzled out.

Among the buildings to look out for are the Dome (built as Hothampton Crescent around 1787), the cubical clock tower in Hotham Park and the brick-and-flint ice house near the library in London Road: it was built for the Hotham estate around 1797.

❯ A few miles up-river from Littlehampton is Arundel, with its Norman castle, medieval church and French Gothic Roman Catholic cathedral set dramatically on the skyline against a backdrop of the Downs. Picturesque streets descend to the Arun, and there's a wildfowl reserve half a mile from the castle. If you don't yet know the town, do allow time to explore it.

A SHRINKING PENINSULA

PAGHAM HARBOUR TO THE WITTERINGS

No part of Sussex feels more provisionally occupied than the broad spit of water-threaded land south of Chichester that is known as the Manhood (or Selsey) Peninsula. To walk this sparsely populated landscape in raw weather is to imagine the sea devouring everything around.

This isn't poetic fancy, because the land has been retreating at between 5 ft (1.5 m) and 20 ft (6 m) a year since the Saxon period, and most of it lies less than 20 ft (6 m) above sea level. Indeed, while planning some limited maintenance of the beach defences between Pagham and the Witterings, the Environment Agency believes the shoreline must inevitably continue to shift further inland year by year. Selsey (once Seal Island) could become cut off again.

It was here that the northern bishop St Wilfrid came ashore in the late seventh century and began to spread Christianity among the South Saxons. His monastery was approached via a causeway and is now far out under the waves: the Normans moved administration of the diocese to dry land at Chichester in 1075, and their cathedral spire stands as a steadfast beacon over these runnelled tracts to the south.

Pagham Harbour

It's difficult to believe that Pagham Harbour was once a leading English port, exporting wool to Europe. Its troubles began as early as the

14th century. In 1341 a huge storm engulfed the hamlet of Charlton (one of several to have disappeared over the centuries) and relentless silting soon brought an end to serious trade.

In 1876, with shingle drift pushing the harbour mouth north-east ever closer to the village of Pagham, a decision was taken to close it off altogether and reclaim the land for agriculture – Pagham Lagoon is its landlocked remnant. Not that it worked, of course. In 1910 the sea broke through the bank, and the water now snakes north-west in two separate channels.

What's bad for the inhabitants is very good indeed for wildlife. These 1,600 acres (650 hectares), are a local nature reserve, with birds congregating in huge numbers on the mudflats and saltmarsh. Terns nest on the shingle; ducks, grebes and waders fish in the lagoon; while the shallow Ferry Pool at the western arm of the harbour (there was a ferry here before the B2145 was carried over the river on a bridge) is reckoned be one of the best 'birding' sites in West Sussex.

Pagham

Parts of Pagham are ancient. The church and the thatched Old Cottage across the road from it date from the early 13th century. Becket's Barn in the Church Farm Holiday Centre is a restored medieval tithe barn and Barton Manor, parts of which are 1,200 years old, is said to be the oldest continuously occupied manor house in England.

By contrast, along West Front Road down at Pagham Beach – and among bungalows and shacks of every description – you'll find a smattering of former railway carriages which managed to survive the clearances of the last war. Local estate agents advertise these humble, sometimes pebbledashed dwellings as 'complete with interesting features' – among them the rows of small windows which give the game away.

This whole beach area of pot-holed roads, shingle tracks and vacant lots (with a few expensive houses beginning to edge themselves in) has an unfinished feel to it. I seem to recall being a little sniffy about Camber Sands, but after the 'nouveau beach' pretentions of so many modern waterfront developments I've come to appreciate areas where nobody has any ambition but to walk the dog, take a dip or clamber into a small boat. You'd be startled to see a man in a suit or a woman in high heels within miles of here. It's shabby, hands-off, away-from-it-all country.

Sidlesham

There was a working tide mill at Sidlesham Quay until Victorian times, and the spot is now wonderfully atmospheric. The walls where the boats moored are still here, although they now contain a tussocky grassland saturated by a narrow remnant of the old mill channel. Across the road is the deep basin (now a garden pond) into which the incoming tide would flow before being released to power the machinery.

Nearby, behind boundary walls of flint and stone, are handsome buildings associated with the once thriving harbour. Some are made of Mixen rock – quarried from a limestone reef which lies off the coast beyond Selsey.

Church Norton

The little chapel by the south-west corner of the harbour is the remnant of a 13th-century building whose nave was removed in the 1860s to create a new church at Selsey. Ecclesiastical law forbids the destruction of a chancel, and that's what survives here in a secluded spot behind the shingle.

The Selsey Tramway

In 1897 the grandly named Hundred of Manhood and Selsey Tramway was opened from south of Chichester down to Selsey – and parts of the embankment are still traceable in the landscape as you walk west of the harbour.

It was one of several light railways (including the Rye and Camber Tramway) devised by Colonel Holman Stephens. The operation was run on a shoestring; the elderly steam trains ran at a maximum speed of 16 mph (26 kph) and were poorly maintained. After the sea broke through in 1910 the track was often flooded and the line was closed for ever just before World War II.

Selsey

What an unpretentious place is Selsey! Approach along the coastline west from Church Norton and you soon come to the lifeboat station, like a tiny pier pavilion at the end of a stretching access ramp lifted on piers above the beach. Continue on round Selsey Bill, the southernmost point in Sussex, and you find yourself at the unheralded end of the main street. There's no drama where it meets the sea: no pier, no promenade – only a small car park in which Linda serves passable pasties from a van.

Selsey is but a fragment of what it once was, but follow the road inland and you'll see that it's happy enough with what it's got. It's a cheap and cheerful place, with a few old cottages at its centre and a sprawl of 20th-century housing beyond.

To its west is the Medmerry area, where four sites run by Bunn Leisure represent the largest conglomeration of holiday caravans anywhere in Europe. You enter the West Sands holiday park by the restored Medmerry tower mill with its four large sweeps.

Fossil bay

The wide expanse of Bracklesham Bay is famous for the fossils washed up on its sand: they come from a bed of soft clay, visible at low tides. Here you can find sharks' teeth and ray plates 45 million years old, together with large brachiopod and gastropod shells which retain just a trace of their original colour. Pre-Roman and Roman coins sometimes turn up, too.

The five-sided tower with attached stair turret which stands proud in the landscape between East and West Wittering (the latter smaller, more upmarket and with its centre a little away from the sea) belongs to Cakeham Manor House, a former medieval palace of the bishops of Chichester.

---

❷ Off Pagham Beach at low tide, half submerged between the breakwaters, you can see Far Mulberry, actually a pier component of one of the 'mulberry harbours' which were towed across to the French coast for the D-Day landings in 1944. This one evidently refused to budge, sank, and has remained here ever since.

LOTS OF YACHTS

CHICHESTER HARBOUR

The sand dunes at East Head, accessible from the beach at West Wittering, form a neat pair of coastal bookends with those we met at the beginning of our journey at Camber. They have the same value to naturalists as a unique and threatened habitat (this is a Site of Special Scientific Interest owned by the National Trust), but they also play a vital role in protecting Chichester Harbour.

The narrow part of the dune system connecting it to the land is known as the hinge, and its breaching would have a major impact on the flow of water through the harbour entrance. A rock berm was installed in 2000, but the defences need constant recharging – and, as ever, there are arguments about how extensive, and expensive, they should be.

For the abundant birdlife here the most important element is mud. One of the many information boards dotted around the harbour explains its richness in language a sailor would understand: in the space taken up by a dinghy you would expect to find 60,000 tiny shrimps or 500 ragworms. A single cubic metre (35 cu ft) of the stuff, according to one (imaginative) local naturalist, has the same calorific value as 16 Mars bars. As a consequence hundreds of thousands of waders tuck into some good meals here between their migrations.

There aren't quite as many boats as this, but it can feel like it as you stroll by the water's edge along one of the narrow inlets. There are 27 sq miles (70 sq km) of navigable water in the harbour (quite a few of them across the border on the Hampshire side) and no fewer than 17 yacht clubs at the last count. Everywhere there are moorings, jetties, quays and boatyards, with boards detailing the state of the tide, the winds and the weather. This was once a thriving port, but today it's given over to pure pleasure.

West Itchenor

The Chichester Channel, the most easterly of the harbour's four main arms, flows all the way to Fishbourne on the south-western fringes of the county town. It takes less than an hour to walk from East Head to Itchenor, where Charles II once kept a yacht.

Here you'll find a couple of boatyards and the headquarters of the Chichester Harbour Conservancy – responsible for everything from navigation, dredging and harbour dues to public access, nature conservation and the management of what is an Area of Outstanding Natural Beauty.

During the season you can take boat trips from here around the harbour, and there's a ferry across to the Bosham side of the creek, west of Bosham Hoe (more jetties and another boatyard).

And do walk or cycle if you can. The villages are reachable by car, but there's nothing to beat a pub lunch or supper after a brisk outing by the waterfront with the smell of the sea in your nostrils. These little settlements are delightful dead-ends, with rows of old cottages dipping down towards hards lined by tarred, weatherboarded relics of earlier sea-faring days.

Two marinas & a canal

At Birdham, a couple of miles further along, we find two contrasting marinas. The unassuming Birdham Pool is probably the oldest in the country and home to several local fishing boats, while the more prestigiously named Chichester Marina has the cluster of magnificent motor yachts and all-gizmos-attached power boats you might expect – although without any of the chi-chi housing that clusters around the basins we've come across further east.

Smaller vessels were going for a mere £20,000 the last time I inspected the advertising hoardings, with gleaming, high-powered gin palaces demanding in the region of £400,000. It costs nothing to look, though.

For a pleasingly shabby contrast turn to where the Chichester Canal runs by. Swans and ducks shake their feathers, trees dip their spreading branches in the water (there's been no traffic here for close on 100 years), and the far bank is lined with houseboats which are much more house than they are boat – floating rectangular boxes which are going nowhere until the rot sets in.

The canal was completed by 1823 as a spur of the Portsmouth to Arundel navigation which, via the Wey & Arun Canal, linked London to the coast. Trade never boomed, however, and the railways soon killed it off altogether.

Dell Quay

For a real touch of a forgotten past, call in at Dell Quay, in medieval times the seventh most important port in the country. (It's said so often that you have to believe it.) Once it exported wool and grain and brought coal, timber and other necessities to the people of Chichester.

Today the old quay itself remains, with some well-restored warehouses next to it, one of them housing the harbour education centre. There's a waterside pub, a fishing and boat club and a sailing club (naturally), but if you'd like to moor your own vessel alongside the pontoon be aware that you can launch only at about two hours either side of high tide: the waters are shallow throughout the harbour.

Fishbourne

From the picturesque mill pond at Fishbourne one path takes you through reedbeds to the shore and another, via a meadow, to the parish church. But the major attraction here, of course, is the Roman palace, tucked away on the edge of a housing estate. That's because the remains of this magnificent building were discovered as recently as 1960, when workmen were digging a trench in the fields – although a cynic will suspect (since a good part of the building lies under houses) that the evidence was first uncovered some time before and kept quiet.

This luxurious pile was probably the home of Togidubnus, a local ruler who threw in his lot with the invading Romans in AD 43 and prospered as a result. The mosaic floors of the north wing are on view under cover, including the celebrated *Cupid on a Dolphin*; there's an excellent museum chock-full of artefacts; and the northern half of the formal garden has been recreated outside.

Bosham

The view of Bosham church from the far bank, with a cluster of flint, brick and tile-hung cottages at the water's edge, is one of the most familiar Sussex images. The church appears in stylised form at the beginning of the Bayeux Tapestry, because it was from here that the future King Harold set sail in 1064 on an ill-fated journey which ended with (according to the Normans) his promising the crown to William.

Don't, on the other hand, believe the fanciful stories connecting Canute to Bosham – although the lapping waters encourage them. Signs state that 'This road floods each tide', and snail-trails of seaweed add their own warning, but the occasional motorist makes the mistake of ignoring the advice.

Thorney Island

And so to our last water-girt landfall in Sussex, the military base which is Thorney Island. Peter Bridgewater describes it in some detail in another book in this series (*An Eccentric Tour of Sussex*), so suffice it to say that you need a security pass to get in and can then enjoy a four-hour stroll around the perimeter past RAF hangars, boatyards and the 12th-century church of St Nicholas.

❯ The Salterns Way is an 11-mile (18-km) cycle route from East Head to the Market Cross at Chichester. It follows rural roads and cycle paths – and the terrain is wonderfully flat.

THE HUMAN CITY

CHICHESTER

The Romans founded Chichester immediately after their invasion of AD 43. It began as a humble garrison from which troops under the future emperor Vespasian could launch their attack on hostile tribes to the west, but it soon became the central market town for a productive corn-growing region, with villas great and small scattered about the landscape. Wherever you dig around the centre of our West Sussex county town you're likely to uncover Roman remains – there's a section of mosaic on view below the cathedral floor.

The typographer and sculptor Eric Gill, who described it as 'the human city, the city of God', particularly admired its layout: 'The plan is clear and clean and rational – a thing of beauty having unity, proportion and clarity.'

Its very orderliness, together with the flatness of the terrain, seems to induce a pervading torpor, but the wide streets are flanked by some fine Georgian buildings, the centre is largly pedestrianised, and a gentle stroll (you can walk right across it in 20 minutes) reveals some attractive little corners and courtyards, especially around the cathedral.

The market cross

There were gates through the Roman walls at the four cardinal points of the compass, and the two main roads met at the centre, as they still do. The ornate octagonal market cross built by Bishop Story has stood at the spot since 1501. It's a riot of ribs, ogee arches, buttresses and finials, with an openwork crown, a small lantern on top and large clock faces on four sides.

Chichester Cathedral

Some are magnificent and austere, but there's a homeliness about Chichester's 12th-century cathedral, with its light-coloured stone and marble, its well-ordered bays, its low vaulting and its gentle Romanesque arches.

On the south wall are two carved stone panels thought to date from 1130, depicting the biblical story of Lazarus being raised from the dead, while a pair of effigies in the north aisle have been given a new lease of life, imaginatively at least, as the centrepiece of Philip Larkin's poem *An Arundel Tomb* – 'What will survive of us is love'.

The late 20th century saw an artistic flowering inside the cathedral. As you enter through the west door, the vivid colours of John Piper's tapestry reredos dance and glow through the medieval stone screen that spans the nave. There's another striking tapestry behind St Richard's shrine, a beautiful font of dark green stone and polished copper by John Skelton, a small Graham Sutherland *noli me tangere* painting of Christ appearing to Mary on the first Easter morning and a glowing stained-glass window in the north aisle by Marc Chagall.

Outside, the massive detached bell tower to the north-west is the only surviving example in England. Round the corner to the south are the cloisters dating from around 1400, with doors into the nave and the retrochoir.

Pallant House

The Pallants area, in the town's south-east quadrant, was cleared of decaying malthouses in the Georgian period to create an elegant crossing of narrow thoroughfares. Two ostriches stand guard on the gateposts outside Pallant House: their sculptor had only a written description to go on, and the building understandably became known as the Dodo House. It's an art gallery, revamped in the past few years by the addition of an unashamedly modern annexe – fittingly, since it specialises in 20th- century art.

A medieval infirmary

St Mary's Hospital, in St Martin's Street, was built around 1290 as an infirmary and chapel sharing a single heavily timbered roof. There were once thousands of hospitals like this throughout medieval Europe, but this is the only English survivor. The usual arrangement was for patients to be bedded down in cubicles against the walls, but self-contained 'flats' were introduced here during the 17th century – and the building still functions as an almshouse today, offering sheltered accommodation to elderly people.

The humane city.

⊃

● The poet William Blake was tried for sedition (and aquitted) at the Guildhall in Priory Park – now a museum. In troubled political times he had a row with a soldier who accused him of declaring support for Napoleon.

INDEX